Stacey Kimmel, MLS
Jennifer Heise, MLS
Editors

Virtual Reference Services: Issues and Trends

Virtual Reference Services: Issues and Trends has been co-published simultaneously as *Internet Reference Services Quarterly*, Volume 8, Numbers 1/2 2003.

Pre-publication REVIEWS, COMMENTARIES, EVALUATIONS . . .

"**A**N IMPRESSIVE COLLECTION of ideas and insights that should assist any library considering the launch of a chat reference service as well as those currently running such services. The experiences of a wide range of institutions and organizations are represented: academic, public, medical, and corporate libraries; library consortia; and the AskERIC service. READERS WILL FIND ALL ASPECTS OF OPERATING A CHAT SERVICE COVERED HERE–everything from planning to promotion to assessment."

Stephen Francoeur, MLS
Information Services Librarian
Baruch College

D1567899

The Haworth Information Press
An Imprint of The Haworth Press, Inc.

Virtual Reference Services: Issues and Trends

Virtual Reference Services: Issues and Trends has been co-published simultaneously as *Internet Reference Services Quarterly*, Volume 8, Numbers 1/2 2003.

Internet Reference Services Quarterly Monographic "Separates"

Below is a list of "separates," which in serials librarianship means a special issue simultaneously published as a special journal issue or double-issue and as a "separate" hardbound monograph. (This is a format which we also call a "DocuSerial.")

"Separates" are published because specialized libraries or professionals may wish to purchase a specific thematic issue by itself in a format which can be separately cataloged and shelved, as opposed to purchasing the journal on an on-going basis. Faculty members may also more easily consider a "separate" for classroom adoption.

"Separates" are carefully classified separately with the major book jobbers so that the journal tie-in can be noted on new book order slips to avoid duplicate purchasing.

You may wish to visit Haworth's website at . . .

http://www.HaworthPress.com

. . . to search our online catalog for complete tables of contents of these separates and related publications.

You may also call 1-800-HAWORTH (outside US/Canada: 607-722-5857), or Fax: 1-800-895-0582 (outside US/Canada: 607-771-0012), or e-mail at:

docdelivery@haworthpress.com

Virtual Reference Services: Issues and Trends, edited by Stacey Kimmel, MLS, and Jennifer Heise, MLS (Vol. 8, No. 1/2, 2003). *Offers practical advice and suggestions for product selection, policy setting, technical support, collaborative efforts, staffing, training, marketing, budgeting, evaluation, and administration.*

Database-Driven Web Sites, edited by Kristin Antelman, MS (Vol. 7, No. 1/2, 2002). *Profiles numerous successful uses of database-driven content to deliver common library services on the Internet.*

Bioterrorism and Political Violence: Web Resources, edited by M. Sandra Wood, MLS, MBA (Vol. 6, No. 3/4, 2002). *Describes how to find reliable information on bioterrorism via the Internet.*

The Challenge of Internet Literacy: The Instruction-Web Convergence, edited by Lyn Elizabeth M. Martin, BA, MLS (Vol. 2, No. 2/3, 1997). *"A source of valuable advice. . . . Recommended for institutions that collect library science materials on a comprehensive level." (Library & Information Science Annual 1999)*

Virtual Reference Services: Issues and Trends

Stacey Kimmel
Jennifer Heise
Editors

Virtual Reference Services: Issues and Trends has been co-published simultaneously as *Internet Reference Services Quarterly*, Volume 8, Numbers 1/2 2003.

The Haworth Information Press
An Imprint of
The Haworth Press, Inc.
New York • London • Oxford

Published by

The Haworth Information Press®, 10 Alice Street, Binghamton, NY 13904-1580 USA

The Haworth Information Press® is an imprint of The Haworth Press, Inc., 10 Alice Street, Binghamton, NY 13904-1580 USA.

Virtual Reference Services: Issues and Trends has been co-published simultaneously as *Internet Reference Services Quarterly*, Volume 8, Numbers 1/2 2003.

The development, preparation, and publication of this work has been undertaken with great care. However, the publisher, employees, editors, and agents of The Haworth Press and all imprints of The Haworth Press, Inc., including The Haworth Medical Press® and Pharmaceutical Products Press®, are not responsible for any errors contained herein or for consequences that may ensue from use of materials or information contained in this work. Opinions expressed by the author(s) are not necessarily those of The Haworth Press, Inc. With regard to case studies, identities and circumstances of individuals discussed herein have been changed to protect confidentiality. Any resemblance to actual persons, living or dead, is entirely coincidental.

Cover design by Brooke R. Stiles.

Library of Congress Cataloging-in-Publication Data

Virtual reference services : issues and trends / Stacey Kimmel, Jennifer Heise, editors.
     p. cm.
   "Co-published simultaneously as Internet reference services quarterly, volume 8, numbers 1/2 2003."
   Includes bibliographical references and index.
   ISBN 0-7890-2044-0 (alk. paper)–ISBN 0-7890-2045-9 (pbk. : alk. paper)
   1. Electronic reference services (Libraries) 2. Electronic reference services (Libraries)–United States–Case studies. 3. Internet in library reference services. 4. Reference services (Libraries)–Information technology. I. Kimmel, Stacey E. II. Heise, Jennifer. III. Internet reference services quarterly.
Z711.45.V577 2003
025.5'24–dc21
                                         2003005365

Indexing, Abstracting & Website/Internet Coverage

This section provides you with a list of major indexing & abstracting services. That is to say, each service began covering this periodical during the year noted in the right column. Most Websites which are listed below have indicated that they will either post, disseminate, compile, archive, cite or alert their own Website users with research-based content from this work. (This list is as current as the copyright date of this publication.)

Abstracting, Website/Indexing Coverage . . . . Year When Coverage Began

- *Annual Bibliography of English Language & Literature "Abstracts Section" (in print, CD-ROM, and online)* **2002**

- *Applied Social Sciences Index & Abstracts (ASSIA) (Online: ASSI via Data-Star) (CDRom: ASSIA Plus) <www.csa.com>* **1996**

- *CINAHL (Cumulative Index to Nursing & Allied Health Literature), in print, EBSCO, and SilverPlatter, Data-Star, and PaperChase. (Support materials include Subject Heading List, Database Search Guide, and instructional video) <www.cinahl.com>* **1996**

- *CNPIEC Reference Guide: Chinese National Directory of Foreign Periodicals* **1996**

- *Computer Literature Index* **1997**

- *Computing Reviews* **1996**

- *Current Cites [Digital Libraries] [Electronic Publishing] [Multimedia & Hypermedia] [Networks & Networking] [General]* **1998**

- *Current Index to Journals in Education* **2002**

(continued)

(continued)

Special Bibliographic Notes related to special journal issues (separates) and indexing/abstracting:

- indexing/abstracting services in this list will also cover material in any "separate" that is co-published simultaneously with Haworth's special thematic journal issue or DocuSerial. Indexing/abstracting usually covers material at the article/chapter level.
- monographic co-editions are intended for either non-subscribers or libraries which intend to purchase a second copy for their circulating collections.
- monographic co-editions are reported to all jobbers/wholesalers/approval plans. The source journal is listed as the "series" to assist the prevention of duplicate purchasing in the same manner utilized for books-in-series.
- to facilitate user/access services all indexing/abstracting services are encouraged to utilize the co-indexing entry note indicated at the bottom of the first page of each article/chapter/contribution.
- this is intended to assist a library user of any reference tool (whether print, electronic, online, or CD-ROM) to locate the monographic version if the library has purchased this version but not a subscription to the source journal.
- individual articles/chapters in any Haworth publication are also available through the Haworth Document Delivery Service (HDDS).

Virtual Reference Services: Issues and Trends

CONTENTS

ABOUT THE EDITORS

Stacey Kimmel, MLS, is Team Leader for Student and General Services in Library & Technology Services at Lehigh University in Bethlehem, Pennsylvania, where she manages a combined library and computing help desk. She has previously held positions at Miami University in Ohio, North Carolina State University, and at the University of North Carolina Health Sciences Library in Chapel Hill. She has worked in library reference, library instruction, and systems, and has completed graduate coursework in technical writing. Her publications include articles on Internet search engines and searching, interdisciplinary research, and virtual reference software. In 1999, she co-authored a bibliography entitled *Interdisciplinary Education: A Guide to Resources.*

Jennifer Heise, MLS, is a Helpdesk Librarian in Library and Technology Services at Lehigh University in Bethlehem, Pennsylvania. She is a co-author (with Stacy Kimmel) of "Being There: Tools for Online Synchronous Reference," published in the November/December 2001 issue of *Online.*

Reading the River:
The State of the Art
of Real-Time Virtual Reference

Jennifer Heise
Stacey Kimmel

SUMMARY. In the face of continuing budget constraints and increased competition from Internet information and "infotainment" sources, libraries are looking for new ways to attract and retain users. Traditional library services, however valuable, are perceived to be less accessible and more inconvenient than Internet alternatives, so librarians have turned their focus to making services available to a new community of online users.

Several years ago, libraries began experimenting with online reference, starting with email reference and moving on to real-time, live, or synchronous reference. What started as a small stream of innovative services has now burgeoned into a river. This volume is an attempt at reading the river–the conditions, signs, and currents–that will help librarians navigate the rapids. By way of an introduction, the editors will briefly sketch the origins of online chat, summarize the contributions, and discuss common themes that have emerged from the contributor viewpoints. *[Article copies available for a fee from The Haworth Document Delivery Service: 1-800-HAWORTH. E-mail address: <docdelivery@haworthpress. com> Website: <http://www.HaworthPress.com> © 2003 by The Haworth Press, Inc. All rights reserved.]*

[Haworth co-indexing entry note]: "Reading the River: The State of the Art of Real-Time Virtual Reference." Heise, Jennifer, and Stacey Kimmel. Co-published simultaneously in *Internet Reference Services Quarterly* (The Haworth Information Press, an imprint of The Haworth Press, Inc.) Vol. 8, No. 1/2, 2003, pp. 1-7; and: *Virtual Reference Services: Issues and Trends* (ed: Stacey Kimmel, and Jennifer Heise) The Haworth Information Press, an imprint of The Haworth Press, Inc., 2003, pp. 1-7. Single or multiple copies of this article are available for a fee from The Haworth Document Delivery Service [1-800-HAWORTH, 9:00 a.m. - 5:00 p.m. (EST). E-mail address: docdelivery@haworthpress.com].

KEYWORDS. Online chat, history, virtual reference trends

GENESIS OF ONLINE CHAT

Instant messaging, or chat, is the online tool *du jour* for millions of Americans. The 2001 *Pew Internet and American Life Project* reported that for teens ages twelve to seventeen, chat is a major communications vehicle.[1] The trend that started with teens and young adults has spread to the workforce, and in 2001, around 18.3 million workers used instant messaging for job-related purposes–a 300% jump from the previous year, according to International Data Corporation.[2] Internet veterans are quick to point out that real-time communication is hardly new; in the 1970s instant messaging was available on mainframe systems, although capabilities were primitive. In the late 1980s Internet Relay Chat (IRC) was introduced, offering multiple channels (many topics) and multiple user discussion. As the Internet developed, messaging systems evolved into chat rooms and complex virtual communities, such as MUDs (multi-user dimension) and MOOs (MUD, object-oriented). Early chat services were used mainly by the computing elite–students and professionals who worked in academic or research settings. Online chat was introduced to the average consumer in the wake of the World Wide Web, with the introduction of ICQ ("I seek you") and, later, instant messaging software. Its inherent appeal, usability, and wide availability spurred rapid growth. For the uninitiated computer user, chat brings the ease and convenience of casual conversation to the desktop.

CHAT AND E-COMMERCE

Before long, online chat software was adapted for electronic commerce, serving as the basis for live online customer service. Companies selling products over the Web found that consumers liked chatting with a live human being for immediate answers to perennial shopping questions such as "Do you have this in my size?" E-commerce chat applications such as HumanClick and e-Gain introduced many consumers to the concept of chat-based assistance on the Web.

THE CASE FOR LIBRARY CHAT

In the last several years, libraries and librarians have begun experimenting with the use of chat technology to provide virtual reference services. Librarians are eager to reach out to online users, who work from nearly anywhere, to access a wider range of resources, with unprecedented autonomy. While librarians applaud the power and convenience of Web accessible resources, they also worry about the average researcher's ability to navigate those resources successfully without guidance. Furthermore, many people already use online chat to talk to friends or to order turtlenecks. If chat is a familiar tool for communicating online, why not use it to offer live library help?

Library users who no longer cross the path of the traditional reference desk find virtual reference appealing on several fronts. First, it's convenient to receive on-the-spot help and answers without having to schlep to the library. Secondly, there are some nice add-ons to basic chat. Even the most humble chat software has features such as page push that are likely to make a favorable impression. For the more reticent library researcher, virtual reference offers the benefits of anonymity and release from the embarrassment of having to ask for help. Stupid questions, if they exist, have no consequences. With all of these advantages, chat, or virtual reference, should be the Next Big Thing for reference service.

Well, that's the theory. Clearly, virtual reference shows early promise. But if there is a bubbling of enthusiasm in the library profession, there is also an undercurrent of pragmatism, even skepticism–are librarians taking on yet another new service with limited staffing and resources? Have the costs and benefits been weighed? How many people will actually make use of this?

This mixture of enthusiasm and concern is reflected in many of the articles in this volume. The contributors respond to both the advocates and the skeptics among us, sharing insights and encouragement while recognizing the very real constraints faced by libraries undertaking this new service. A summary of the article contributions is below.

CONTRIBUTORS AND TOPICS

This volume starts with Lipow's thoughtful and powerfully written essay. She cheers on those who have entered the realm of virtual services and advocates a revisioning of reference services, calling for reference professionals to move beyond the library ("the librarian has left the building") to reach users where they are doing their work.

The bottom line for virtual reference is user satisfaction. Barr, Conley, and Goode examine virtual reference from the perspective of continuous quality improvement (CQI) principles and concepts. The Kano Model of user satisfaction can help libraries to view virtual reference services in the context of customer expectations as they change over time.

Public library systems are represented in this volume. Cichanowicz reports on the adoption of virtual reference service at Suffolk Cooperative Library System in New York. She advocates a user-centered perspective and describes how this perspective informs decisions about procedures and service.

Many of the contributors discuss staffing, but one article focuses on this topic. Ronan shares advice and experience from the University of Florida and a survey of other libraries. She discusses selection of staff, structuring the work environment, scheduling, and other issues.

Sweet, Lisa, and Colston offer a close look at collaborative virtual reference in the state of New Jersey. They describe in detail not only the development of the Q and A NJ initiative but also the participation of Newark and Wayne Public libraries.

Most libraries seem to opt for established commercial virtual reference products that offer text-based chat as the central communications tool. Wanserski chronicles the development of a virtual reference service product that combines voice over IP, integration with digital collections, and a sophisticated communication environment for end-users and librarians. Readers get an insider's view of progress and setbacks encountered while testing and developing innovative software in a corporate partnership.

Beyond the initial implementation, there are unique issues for ongoing management of virtual reference services. Ciccone and VanScoy move beyond issues of implementation, sharing the post-implementation experience of North Carolina State University. In particular they address issues of call volume, difficult users, training and quality assessment, and service improvement.

Colvin's overview of the virtual reference initiatives in Florida libraries gives a broad panoramic view of the processes and options being pursued by a variety of libraries. The success of virtual reference initiatives at university, community college, and public library systems has driven plans for statewide and regional collaboration.

McClellan offers the unique perspective of a medical and dental library participating in a multi-type library service that assists a diverse clientele. Insights on how a health sciences library contributes to, and benefits from, this initiative are outlined. She includes a discussion of budgeting, training, administration/coordination, morale, marketing, and local/remote user reaction.

In the library literature there are few articles on virtual reference in special libraries. Martin's article on virtual reference services at The Boeing Company provides insight into digital services in general, and virtual reference specifically, at a special library.

One of the challenges for librarians is evaluation of virtual reference services. Belanger, Lankes and Shostack offer a model and framework for collecting statistical data in a virtual reference service, with AskERIC's implementation as the example. They provide examples of what data can be collected as well as how to interpret and use the results.

One of the contributions to this volume focuses on the nature of the virtual reference interaction. Does a real reference interaction take place in the context of virtual reference? Do users and librarians follow the same pattern as in face-to-face interactions? To answer these questions, Marsteller and Mizzy conduct a thorough analysis of chat transcripts from Carnegie Mellon University.

Virtual reference is often one of several services offered from library Web pages, and Fagan and Desai's article offers insight into how users interact with these services. They offer an illuminating comparison of Southern Illinois University-Carbondale's use of the library Web site search tool versus use of the virtual reference service on that site.

EMERGING THEMES

Among the contributions it was possible to identify many common threads, or emerging themes. Librarians share similar concerns, challenges, successes, and hopes for virtual reference, and it would be tedious to note them all. However, the major themes are outlined below.

Terminology

The authors of these articles make use of a bewildering variety of phrases to refer to virtual reference service in their texts: real-time reference, live online reference, chat reference, instant messaging reference, synchronous online reference, virtual reference, VR, and more. From this sampling of papers it appears that there is no common vocabulary among professionals to refer to this kind of service. In branding and marketing a library's chat service, there is similar variation in how the service is identified to users, but with the added confusion of identifying, or not identifying, the name of the underlying software product. Most libraries have elected to use a unique name different from the product name. Many of the contributors reported difficulty in arriving at a name descriptive enough to convey the kind of service offered. One library reported that users were startled to connect to a live human. Another library's transaction log showed that users confused the Web site search tool with the virtual reference link. Attempts to clarify the service to users were numerous. Some libraries polled users to help name the service, while others tried several names in pilot testing. Clearly the immediacy and interactive nature of this service are difficult to convey to a naïve user.

Administrative Issues

Technical problems in virtual reference service delivery are conspicuously absent from these reports. Instead, authors devote considerable time and attention to the many administrative considerations, including staff selection, scheduling, training, and motivation; budgeting; legal and ethical issues; policies and procedures; interlibrary cooperation; hours of operation; user interface design; and more. Each library handles these issues differently and in ways that are hard to characterize succinctly. Of the administrative concerns, staffing was the most-discussed in these articles. One common nugget of advice for libraries with limited staff and budgets is to "start small," with a pilot, limited hours, or by offering virtual reference services during consultation hours.

Software

Many different brands of software are being used to implement real-time online reference. The Library Systems and Services, LLC (LSSI) Virtual Reference Desk and divine's Virtual Reference Desk represent the luxury line of sophisticated and customizable software. Mid-range products such as LivePerson are widely used, however, with positive results. Other libraries have used lesser-known alternatives–using versatile communications tools adapted to virtual reference, open source products and/or locally developed applications, or in one case, a high-end online reference environment developed through corporate partnership.

Collaboration

Statewide, regional, and local collaborative virtual reference efforts are flourishing, as evidenced by the success of Q and A NJ and Suffolk Cooperative Library System's LiveLibrarian. Organizations with multiple libraries, such as Boeing Company and University of Wisconsin, are also jointly staffing and coordinating virtual reference services. Given the concern over staffing and hours of coverage, interlibrary cooperation will likely be a strong focus in virtual reference development.

Analysis

Some virtual reference services have been in operation long enough to accumulate considerable data. Managers have begun to analyze these records, logs, and statistics, and in this volume they share how services are evaluated through usage data, question content, surveys, and anecdote/case studies (to name a few). Results of these evaluations help to distinguish the myth versus reality of virtual reference. Do we really need to staff late night hours? Do traditional reference and query negotiation happen in a virtual environment? What kind of questions are users asking? Evaluation of services is a critical component of the projects described in these pages.

CONCLUSION

Judging from the contributions in this volume, virtual reference is an established and growing part of library service. Future trends will surely include greater integration with other university and library online services (e.g., portals, courseware, databases, and document delivery). Another likely trend is moving the service beyond the desktop text chat environment to include mobile devices, and also expanding to other forms of communication such as videoconferencing. Increased interlibrary collaboration is all but a given as it offers the benefits of enhanced service and cost sharing. The editors hope that this volume will offer readers insight into the benefits and challenges of providing virtual reference services.

NOTES

1. Amanda Lenhart, Lee Rainie, and Oliver Lewis. *Teenage Life Online: The rise of the instant-message generation and the Internet's impact on friendships and family relationships.* Pew Internet and American Life Project: Washington, D.C. Available at <http://www.pewinternet.org/reports/pdfs/PIP_Teens_Report.pdf>. Accessed. September 30, 2002.

2. Mark Chediak, Instant Messaging Gets Serious, *Red Herring*, September 1, 2001. Available: <http://www.redherring.com/mag/issue103/1300020130.html>. Accessed: September 30, 2002.

The Librarian Has Left the Building–
But To Where?

Anne Grodzins Lipow

SUMMARY. This paper applauds the recent growth of virtual point-of-need reference services in libraries as a step in the direction of paying attention to users who, now that they have handy commercial alternatives, won't ask a question at the physical reference desk from within the library building or no longer come into the building. However, like the "horseless carriage" analogy, we seem to be using the new technology to maintain the status quo. The author argues for regarding virtual reference service as a starting point to transform ready reference services altogether, raising libraries and librarians to a new level of importance within their communities. *[Article copies available for a fee from The Haworth Document Delivery Service: 1-800-HAWORTH. E-mail address: <docdelivery@haworthpress.com> Website: <http://www.HaworthPress.com> © 2003 by The Haworth Press, Inc. All rights reserved.]*

KEYWORDS. Rethinking reference, virtual reference service, redefining professional work

DEVELOPMENTS IN VIRTUAL REFERENCE

The sudden sprout of virtual reference services in libraries is a wonderful development. It represents an attention to the library user who has migrated to

Anne Grodzins Lipow (anne@library-solutions.com) is Founder and Director of Library Solutions Institute and Press <http://www.library-solutions.com>.

[Haworth co-indexing entry note]: "The Librarian Has Left the Building–But To Where?" Lipow, Anne Grodzins. Co-published simultaneously in *Internet Reference Services Quarterly* (The Haworth Information Press, an imprint of The Haworth Press, Inc.) Vol. 8, No. 1/2, 2003, pp. 9-18; and: *Virtual Reference Services: Issues and Trends* (ed: Stacey Kimmel, and Jennifer Heise) The Haworth Information Press, an imprint of The Haworth Press, Inc., 2003, pp. 9-18. Single or multiple copies of this article are available for a fee from The Haworth Document Delivery Service [1-800-HAWORTH, 9:00 a.m. - 5:00 p.m. (EST). E-mail address: docdelivery@haworthpress.com].

http://www.haworthpress.com/store/product.asp?sku=J136
© 2003 by The Haworth Press, Inc. All rights reserved.
10.1300/J136v08n01_02

other information services, most notably, to other question-answering services. Virtual reference begins to address a critical issue that has been with us for years but one that we have refused to face: clients' preference for convenience over quality. In making it easier for users to opt for a quality service, reference librarians are asking not "What can we do to get people with questions to come to the library?" but instead, "How can we bring the service to where our users are when they have a question?" And their answer is: to be "in your face";[1] to be so "there," alongside Google's search engine and a live commercial reference service such as Webhelp, that when quality matters, the library is the service of choice. Dozens of vendors have sprung up overnight and their customer service software has been tailored to the reference environment. They are evidence that the business world believes that libraries are beginning to fill a need that commercial virtual question-answering services proved beyond a doubt existed.

So I applaud my pioneering colleagues. You have left the physical building and set up shop in cyberspace. You have taken one giant step toward your distant users (who may be somewhere in your library!). And I give extra points to colleagues in libraries providing round-the-clock service, sharing the load with other libraries in your region or across time zones, or with other libraries of the same type. You have taken the bold extra step of trusting that reference librarians in other libraries can give quality service to your clientele, and that you can reciprocate. You are even comfortable seeing (because you can monitor the logs) that the "other" librarians know when to refer clients back to their home libraries. Best of all, you complete the convenience circle by providing ready reference service not only *where* your client with a question is, but also *whenever* your client has a question.[2] I am especially impressed with the libraries that are exploring effective techniques to promote their services.

Of course, libraries have been serving distant users for a long time, beginning with book mobile service and home deliveries to disabled people. Since the late 1980s, they have been providing remote access, first to the public catalogs via telnet and then to all of the libraries' electronic resources. However, until now, the rest of your library–including your reference service–has been closed to people who, for one reason or another, do not or cannot come to the library during your business hours. Today, many libraries not only make reference service available from afar, but also other services that had heretofore been available only to walk-in users, such as story hour, registering for a library card, and classes in information literacy. To make all of these services available to people who do not have Internet access at home, some libraries have installed "e-branches" or library workstations in shopping malls and other public places. These libraries deserve special kudos for moving closer to fulfilling their unique core mission: equal access to information for the entire community.

Despite these advances, to the degree that we change nothing about the content of the work itself, we are missing the opportunity to take a giant leap for libraries. Except in the few libraries that have eliminated the reference desk altogether, we haven't used this change as an opportunity to rethink point-of-need reference service: neither its conceptual framework, nor the practice of ready reference work itself. We still have one foot stuck in the old reference desk, and there is no sign that we are aware of the consequences of our restricted vision.

SAME SERVICE, NEW TECHNOLOGY

"Same old service; brand new technology," explained a manager of a busy networked 24/7 virtual reference service in a talk to a large audience of librarians who had recently launched or were about to embark on such a service. She was probably trying to allay their fears about the unknowns of such a major change. However, in doing so, she inadvertently closed the door to new concepts and opportunities that would be the prerequisites for making fundamental and, I believe, necessary, changes in our profession.

Her words reminded me of what we librarians said decades ago to our users who regarded the newfangled online public catalog with great trepidation. "Not to worry," we reassured them, "this catalog is just like your old friend the card catalog. . . ." The trouble with that comparison is that it encouraged users to maintain the same mental model of the online catalog as they held of the card catalog, whose searchability was based on very limited concepts. Also, such a comparison risked the likelihood that users' misconceptions about the card catalog (and they had many!) would be carried over to the online catalog where they would continue search habits that should have long before been broken. I'm always unpleasantly surprised when today I come across a library's Web site, on the homepage of which is a link to "the online card catalog." I can't help but wonder if in those libraries both the users and the librarians are stuck in a previous century.

We seem in denial that an ever-growing camp of administrators believes that search engines and commercial live reference services can replace reference librarians.[3] Too often, our answer to the declining number of questions asked at the physical desk is, "We should count differently." We remain aloof from discussions about what exactly is "professional" work when paraprofessionals also answer questions at the reference desk, working both alongside librarians and independently.

REFERENCE DESK? WHAT'S THAT?

It is surely our narrow concept of our work that has kept us from solving a problem we've known about for decades: clients' ignorance about or unwillingness to use the reference desk. I regularly survey the users and non-users of public and academic libraries. To my question, "To what extent do you use the reference desk?", two common replies are "Reference desk? What's that?" and "Never. I don't want to bother them." In one library, where the reference desk was not readily visible, a few answered that they use the service frequently. However, when I asked them to lead me to the desk where they received reference service, I was taken to the circulation desk. When I report these findings to the library reference staff, to my astonishment, they are never surprised; they recognize the responses very well–and even add more, such as the reference librarian who said, "I am sure that the people who come to the desk are those with whom I've made eye contact." Barbara Fister recently discovered that many students are reluctant to come to their academic library's reference desk because they'd "face the humiliation of being seen asking for help in public."[4] How can it be, I ask you, that with this anecdotal knowledge, you haven't solved the puzzle? If your reference service were a business, the problem of people needing but not using the service would have been dealt with head on and solved long ago, or it would be closed down.

VIRTUAL REFERENCE AND THE HORSELESS CARRIAGE

For those of you offering virtual reference service, what do you know about the people using your service and about those who don't? What evidence do you have that your strategies for letting your clientele know about your service are working? How aware are you of the usability of your Website and the degree to which it encourages or discourages use of your service? Anthropologist Bonnie Nardi claims that reference work, important as it is, is invisible to reference librarians as well as to their clients. She argues convincingly that unless you make visible the complexities and impact of your work, you are in danger of becoming extinct.[5] So it seems logical that to continue business as usual, leaving unexamined the nature of and need for reference work, is to maintain reference work in an invisible cloak.

In short, amidst all the change that virtual reference represents, we remain tied tightly to the status quo. Clifford Lynch expresses best the concern we should all have over this narrow approach to virtual reference service. In the "Foreword" of *The Virtual Reference Librarian's Handbook*, he writes:

I will admit that I sometimes worry that virtual reference may be too limiting a vision, too literal a translation of the practices of physical libraries to the networked world, too much of a view through a rear-view mirror. "Virtual reference" has a bit of an echo with concepts like "horseless carriage," and I find myself wondering whether it may be more productive to think more broadly about network-based library services and library presence in evolving network-based communities.[6]

To which I would add: this "too literal a translation" of the physical reference desk to the networked world is a translation from a reference service that wasn't justifiable to begin with! As I noted in a white paper presented at a RUSA program at an ALA Conference in Atlanta, June 2002:

If the truth be known, as a place to get help in finding information, the reference desk was never a good idea. A reference librarian standing behind a desk waiting for someone to say, "I can't find what I'm looking for; can you help?" might be justifiable if, as is the case with other service professionals, that librarian was the reason the person came to the building to begin with. But reference librarians have not served so central a function. They have stood ready to help "just in case"–just in case navigating the building isn't clear, just in case the catalog doesn't produce wanted results, just in case the collections seem not to contain the desired material or information. In short, reference service–in particular point-of-need reference service–has been an afterthought, something to be considered after the building's signage or the finding aids or the collections fail the user.[7]

Not only do librarians play a passive role in serving their clientele, but they are woefully uncritical about their work and the service they give. Measures of success have focused on numbers and anecdotes. Articles in our professional journals analyze the effectiveness of various question-handling techniques in order to improve the answers given to those who ask questions, but what about those who don't ask? Again, from the above white paper:

The external appearances have led us to believe the service works fine: there is enough traffic at the desk to keep us busy most of the time, and our clients express their sincere gratitude for the personalized assistance they received. Not wanting to disturb a good thing, librarians have been silent in the knowledge that people wander throughout the library needing help but never get to the reference desk. Librarians have done little more than bemoan the laziness of users who sit at an Internet-connected computer 20 feet from the reference desk but ask their questions of a commercial online reference service, where they get faulty answers.[8]

Luckily, virtual reference service is still very much in the developmental stage. Before it becomes a fait accompli, it would be wise to view virtual reference as an opening to rethink point-of-need reference service altogether–how it should be delivered, who should deliver it, and to whom should it be delivered. That won't be an easy task. Librarians will need to begin thinking of themselves as working in one node of a vast global network comprised of the world's libraries, regarding their work as based not in their building but independent of their building.[9] As the networks of virtual reference services grow, it will become increasingly important to understand the differences between the relevance of the local library to the local community and that of the local library to beyond the community. It will become especially necessary to understand reference work as Bonnie Nardi hopes it will be understood, to be able to eliminate the parts that others, including search engines, can handle.

RESHAPING PROFESSIONAL WORK

Now is an especially auspicious time for examining and thinking beyond the status quo. The 2002-2003 president of the American Library Association, Maurice (Mitch) Freedman, is devoting his year in office to launching a campaign to promote better salaries for all library workers. Unionization will make a difference in individual libraries that have the bargaining power to be listened to. However, if this campaign is to be successful throughout the profession, it will be necessary to wage the battle on two other fronts: the law, and established convention.

The Law: Equal Pay for Equal Work

It is well known that as a female-typed occupation, both men and women librarians earn approximately 67% of people in male-typed occupations requiring similar backgrounds of education and experience (analyst, systems designer, instructional designer, marketer, accountant, city planner, architect, etc.). So it will be important to make comparisons between the pay of librarians and that of comparable male-typed occupations. And it will be equally important to be able to differentiate the work of paraprofessionals who work at the reference desk for lower pay than the librarians delivering the same service in the same place.

Established Convention: Scarcity and Impact

It is an observable fact that the professional who receives (and is regarded as deserving) higher pay is one whose special body of knowledge isn't readily available. As Joan Frye Williams observes, higher-paid professionals are those who make themselves scarce.[10] Another yardstick of work that translates into higher pay is its degree of impact: the more far-reaching, the higher the pay. If reference librarians redesigned their work, they would be in a unique position within the profession to address pay issues in the context of their availability and impact.

What follows, then, are two questions, intended to contribute to a discussion about a fundamental reshaping of reference services. I have no answers to these questions—only early thoughts about issues to grapple with in arriving at answers.

Question 1: What constitutes "professional" work?

An honest evaluation of the questions asked at your face-to-face reference desk will reveal that very small percentages are of the type that requires an MLS to answer. But at a time when where the library's money is going is under scrutiny, it isn't acceptable that you are answering "How do I renew this book?" or "What are your hours tomorrow?" or even "Do you have this title?" Reference desks staffed by well-trained paraprofessionals have proven that today they can answer questions that once only experienced reference librarians could handle.

How much better your job description would look if, instead of "works ten to fifteen hours/week on the reference desk," it said, in relation to ready reference:

- On the premise that every question asked at the desk is evidence of the library's failure to be self-evident to the client, analyzes point-of-need questions with the view to eliminating categories of questions; suggests methods to accomplish this; and participates in the implementation of approved methods. [Ensuring a continued sense of the changing nature of clients' questions may entail working two or so hours a week at the reference or information desk.]
- Maintains on-call hours to receive referrals from the Information Desk.
- Provides in-depth consultations by appointment.
- Keeps abreast of the skills and training that are needed to provide front-line ready reference service, whether face-to-face or virtual, and

participates in the design and delivery of training programs that upgrade the skills of appropriate staff.

An important part of redefining professional work is to determine what structures of reference services would best meet the needs of diverse clientele. I am impressed with the libraries that have established tiered services in recognition that one size doesn't fit all. Again, your job description would read so much better if, instead of, "provides point-of-need reference services to a diverse clientele," it instead read:

- Analyzes the community's library use patterns as well as the information needs of people who don't or can't come to the library, and designs and implements new services that fill those needs, such as home delivery of library materials and services targeted to special-interest groups.
- Participates in joint councils and advisory groups comprised of non-library organizations and leaders within the community.

Question 2: How do we take advantage of networking technology, librarians' expertise that taken together covers all categories of knowledge, and the already existing regional, national, and international library organizational structures to improve reference services to our own clientele?

An essential contribution to the continued health of libraries would be the restructuring of the relationship among and staffing of libraries' reference services–both the point-of-need services and the more delayed levels of service. Certainly the Internet makes it feasible–perhaps mandatory–to break down the walls that separate libraries, redraw the geographical boundaries of staffing the virtual reference desk and move toward a fully networked system.

With the Library of Congress-initiated Global Reference Network (GRN), we're off to a good start. GRN's embryonic QuestionPoint, a digital reference service that rests on LC's cooperative venture with OCLC, holds out the promise of providing the leadership and support that will spin the web linking the world's libraries. QuestionPoint's model is: go your own way, the way that best meets the needs of your clientele. You can be an individual library using whatever software you choose, or a consortium of libraries, sharing the load and all using the same software, whatever is on the market (including QuestionPoint Local/Regional). When you need more–whether a special expertise or a time zone, you switch to QuestionPoint Global, staffed 24/7 by librarians around the world.[11]

Of QuestionPoint's many ambitious goals, two are critical to providing the infrastructure that will blur the geographical boundaries separating libraries:

(a) "respond to, track and manage reference questions from patrons via the Web" (at present, the questions can be submitted only by librarians on behalf of their patrons), and (b) to operate in many languages (at present, all communication is in English). I look forward to the day when we can usurp Kinko's slogan:

1100 branches
20,000 people
All connected

Libraries would, of course, use much larger numbers.

In sum, librarians have begun to move the reference desk beyond the walls of their building. Now their minds and bodies need to move, too, toward changing a status quo that is becoming outdated. The result will surely be an image and reality of libraries and librarians raised to a new level of importance within their communities and beyond. A significant byproduct of such a dramatic change will be a stronger position from which to demand better pay.

NOTES

1. Anne Lipow, "In-Your-Face Reference Service." *Library Journal* 124, no. 13 (August 1999): 50-2.

2. Judging from my observations, to have less than 24/7 service seems to keep traffic low. Clients' *perception* that you may not be open, even when you are, is enough to discourage use. It takes only once trying you when you are closed for the client to conclude that it isn't worth memorizing your hours. Similarly, clients' perception of the delay in response time–even when you routinely respond within two or three hours–may be the chief reason that 99% of e-mail reference services aren't overwhelmed with traffic.

3. For a thought-provoking analysis of reference work and what needs to be done, see Jerry Campbell, "Clinging to Traditional Reference Services: An Open Invitation to libref.com." *Reference & User Services Quarterly* 39, no. 3 (Spring 2000): 223-7.

4. Barbara Fister, "Fear of Reference." *Chronicle of Higher Education* 48, no. 40 (June 14, 2002): B20. The author concludes–erroneously, in my opinion–that virtual reference is not the answer. She apparently has missed the testimonies reported of the many people who say they feel more comfortable asking questions of an email or live virtual service because of the privacy and anonymity the medium affords.

5. Bonnie Nardi, "Information Ecologies." Keynote address at the Library of Congress Institute "Reference Service in a Digital Age," June 30, 1998, Library of Congress, Washington, D.C. Available: <http://lcweb.loc.gov/rr/digiref/archive/nardi.html>. Accessed: July 17, 2002.

6. Clifford Lynch, "Foreword," In *The Virtual Reference Librarian's Handbook*, by Anne Grodzins Lipow (New York, NY: Neal-Schuman), 2003.

7. Anne Lipow, "Point-of-Need Reference Service: No Longer an Afterthought" A white paper presented at a RUSA program, ALA Conference, Atlanta, June 2002. Available: <http://www.ala.org/rusa/forums/lipow_forum.html>. Accessed: July 17, 2002.

8. Lipow, "Point-of-Need Reference Service: No Longer an Afterthought."

9. Just as a type of medical doctor called "hospitalist" is one whose work is confined to hospitals, so, too, "librarian" implies that our work is limited to the library building. Some say that if we called ourselves something other than the name of the building we work in, we would free our minds to think about our work differently.

10. One of many keen observations by Joan Frye Williams in her presentation, "Reprofessionalizing Librarianship" at Amigos Conference, Dallas, 1 May 2002.

11. For more information about QuestionPoint, start at the Global Reference Network Homepage, Library of Congress. Available: <http://www.loc.gov/rr/digiref/>. Accessed: July 17, 2002.

Chat Is Now:
Administrative Issues

Belinda Barr
Jerome Conley
Joanne Goode

SUMMARY. In this article, the authors explore the administrative issues that surround the introduction of a chat service into an academic library community. The issues are examined from a customer service viewpoint addressed through the Kano Model, developed by Dr. Noriaki Kano and rooted in Continuous Quality Improvement (CQI) and Total Quality Management (TQM). The authors discuss how academic libraries can apply the Kano Model to the virtual reference environment. The authors also discuss the importance of balancing customer service with the limited resources available to academic libraries introducing a new service. *[Article copies available for a fee from The Haworth Document Delivery Service: 1-800-HAWORTH. E-mail address: <docdelivery@haworthpress.com> Website: <http://www.HaworthPress.com> © 2003 by The Haworth Press, Inc. All rights reserved.]*

KEYWORDS. Administrative issues, chat reference, digital reference, customer service, Kano Model

Belinda Barr (bbarr@lib.muohio.edu) is Head of Information Services, King Library, Jerome Conley (jconley@lib.muohio.edu) is Coordinating Head of Special Libraries, and Joanne Goode (jgoode@lib.muohio.edu) is Head of Brill Science Library, all at Miami University, Oxford, OH 45056.

[Haworth co-indexing entry note]: "Chat Is Now: Administrative Issues." Barr, Belinda, Jerome Conley, and Joanne Goode. Co-published simultaneously in *Internet Reference Services Quarterly* (The Haworth Information Press, an imprint of The Haworth Press, Inc.) Vol. 8, No. 1/2, 2003, pp. 19-25; and: *Virtual Reference Services: Issues and Trends* (ed: Stacey Kimmel, and Jennifer Heise) The Haworth Information Press, an imprint of The Haworth Press, Inc., 2003, pp. 19-25. Single or multiple copies of this article are available for a fee from The Haworth Document Delivery Service [1-800-HAWORTH, 9:00 a.m. - 5:00 p.m. (EST). E-mail address: docdelivery@haworthpress.com].

10.1300/J136v08n01_03

INTRODUCTION

While some libraries are just beginning to think about, or to implement, a virtual real-time reference service, many libraries have already completed pilot projects and are integrating the service into everyday routines.[1] Now is a critical time for library administrators to stop and think about how the library profession is addressing digital reference service. It is difficult for many in the reference profession to believe that traditional face-to-face reference service may not continue as the core, definitive means of providing reference services in an academic environment. It would be much easier to accept this new form of reference service as an "add on" to traditional services or even as just the next logical step after e-mail reference. To do this would not only be a mistake, it would be a missed opportunity. R. David Lankes presents some very thought provoking observations in his editorial aptly titled, "Birth Cries of Digital Reference," which concludes with the observation, "Readers . . . should heed the cries of an infant digital reference field, or they will be deafened by the roars of the coming reference revolution."[2] Digital reference is here. Libraries that do not embrace this new challenge risk losing their customers, who will turn to other interactive information providers and services to meet their needs. It is, therefore, imperative that library administrators find ways to offer interactive online assistance to their library communities and to support current staff in their pursuit of initiatives that reach customers online, in real-time.

Library administrators face numerous issues when providing support for digital assistance initiatives, such as making software and hardware decisions, determining hours of service, soliciting staff involvement, and offering training. Real-time digital assistance is yet another service that, although critical, can be impeded by overwhelmed staff and tight budgets. The Kano Model is a tool administrators can employ to identify customer needs. Administrators must then attempt to balance customer needs with staff concerns in the ever-changing environment of providing information.

THE KANO MODEL

Dr. Noriaki Kano of Tokyo Rike University developed the Kano Model of Customer Satisfaction in the late 1970s. This model is a tool used for measuring and validating customer needs and is composed of three features of customer satisfaction.[3] Each feature connects to some degree of fulfillment:

- Basic features are those that are so obvious to the customer they are taken for granted when executed perfectly. However, when executed poorly, customers experience great dissatisfaction that may be expressed as complaints. Basic features are so elemental that they do not generate excitement or loyalty. An example of a Basic library feature is the expectation that libraries offer online catalogs.

- Performance features are those features that customers can articulate and that slightly increase customer satisfaction. For example, online research databases can be thought of as Performance features.
- Excitement features address customer needs of which the customer is not aware. They are unexpected, impress customers, greatly increase their satisfaction, and can generate loyalty. Excitement features generate satisfaction even if execution is modest. At this point in time, online real-time chat is an example of an Excitement feature.

Kano determined that two outcomes emerge when applying his model:

1. Excitement features become Basic features over time.
2. Minimal customer needs must be met before offering Performance or Excitement features.

THE KANO MODEL IN LIBRARIES

As service organizations, libraries have increasingly become focused on customer satisfaction. Most libraries already follow the principles of the Kano Model instinctively when introducing new services because the core of most libraries is quality customer service and customer satisfaction. A library illustration of the Kano Model in action is the transition from the simplistic online public access catalog (OPAC) to the sophisticated interactive online services and products. In this scenario, customers' Basic needs and the first element of the Kano Model were met with the simple OPAC. The second element, the Performance feature of the Kano Model, was the unveiling of a Web-based system that included the OPAC and numerous databases. The final stage of the Model is the Excitement feature that is demonstrated with the introduction of a system that offers library staff the means to communicate virtually, in real-time with remote users. Conversely, the early, simple OPAC was an Excitement feature for many customers when it was first introduced. As the Kano Model predicted, as time passed, excitement about the online catalog transitioned to a Basic customer feature for libraries.

Another illustration of the Kano Model is the transition from traditional reference to the virtual reference environment. For Miami University Libraries the transition began in 1994 when the library Web system, MiamiLINK, was unveiled. MiamiLINK displaced the OPAC as the new Excitement feature. With the new system, more and more products and full-text resources were offered through the Web. Librarians perceived a need for an easy, interactive, real-time method to reach remote researchers as the number of users who no longer needed to set foot in a library increased. Although the Libraries offered an email service, it did not meet this interactive, real-time need. Once again, as the Kano Model suggests, the library found itself facing a new customer need for immediate help when using online library resources. Chat service was born to meet this need.

IMPLEMENTATION ISSUES

When planning to introduce a chat service at Miami, implementation issues fell into three distinct categories: administrative support and allies; identification of software, hours, and staff involvement; and training.

Administrative Support and Allies

In an ideal world, frontline staff would approach library administrators with the suggestion to offer a chat service. However, if that does not happen, library administrators should identify those library staff members who are excited by new ideas and services and who can serve as core allies and advocates for the new service. While the bottom-up model is more desirable, the top-down model can be effective because librarians have a natural desire to meet the needs of their customers, and service to remote customers is an important issue. Once a decision has been made to offer a chat service, administrators have an obligation to offer support and positive reinforcement as library staff members develop the new service. It is essential for administrators to articulate a vision, break barriers as they arise, balance customer needs with available resources, and demonstrate a willingness to sculpt[4] position responsibilities.

Identification of Software

The first issue to explore is the software necessary to offer a chat service. The exploration may run the gamut, from free services like America Online Instant Messenger to low cost software or open source solutions like RAKIM,[5] to high cost commercial call center software like eLibrarian from Digi-Net Technologies, Inc. A software recommendation will be dependent upon the funding available, the type of service required by customers, the functions staff would like to have at hand, the stability of software, and whether to use local or commercial servers. When considering the software recommendation, library administrators must always balance customer needs with library resources, including the talents of current staff who can create or modify software to meet the needs of their customers and staff.

At Miami, frontline librarians passionately articulated that the library needed to offer a real-time service or risk losing users to the burgeoning commercial information service providers. Library administration acknowledged the need for a virtual reference service but recognized that the cost of purchasing commercial call center software was prohibitive. The libraries solved the dilemma by tapping into the talents of an existing staff member who quickly created an open source product, RAKIM. The libraries were now positioned to offer a limited real-time chat service in the fall of 2000 and consequently fill both the needs of librarians and customers. Although the software was initially unsophisticated, it was stable and functional enough to support the new chat service. The new chat service became an Excitement feature for customers. As the Kano Model suggests, it generated customer satisfaction even though execution was modest.

After using the software for one semester, librarians as well as customers quickly moved to the Kano Performance stage of customer satisfaction by expressing a desire for a more robust system. The next release enhanced the original features and met many of the Performance needs. The Excitement features of the original software then became Basic features of customer satisfaction. When the developer unveils the next generation of RAKIM, the librarian and customers will again most likely attain the Excitement stage of customer satisfaction. Inevitably, the new software features will migrate into the Basic realm.

Service Hours, Staff Involvement, and Staff Training

The next issues to examine are service hours, staff involvement, and staff training. These issues are multifaceted, and administrators must be aware of factors intertwined with each issue. For instance, hours of service may be the same as in-house reference hours, more limited than reference hours, extended beyond reference hours, or influenced by a consortial chat service. The service may be offered from an existing service point, from home or an office, through a contract service, or by a combination of these approaches. If customer needs are kept in the forefront when scheduling the service, hours offered may vary from typical service hours. Library administrators may find Bernie Sloan's evaluation of the Ready for Reference project of interest when determining hours of operation. Sloan's analysis states that, "less than half (43.4%) of all activity took place between the 'typical' business hours of 8 a.m. and 5 p.m."

Interestingly he also found that, "the wee hours of the morning (1 a.m. to 6 a.m.) don't generate much activity at all . . . "[6]

Administrators need to consult with managers to determine whether staffing a new chat service will be considered part of primary reference duties or will be secondary to reference responsibilities. This decision will have a significant impact on the availability of staff as well as on how the service is viewed by the staff. Administrators may need to find creative ways to staff the service, such as integrating staff members who do not currently have reference responsibilities, hiring new staff, or training undergraduate and/or graduate students. Hopefully, these staff members will contribute to the success of the service by bringing fresh perspectives and unique skill sets.

An initial and ongoing training program is crucial for the success of the service. This program should involve not only formal training, but also informal sessions where staff members can experiment and gain comfort with the software and the chat environment. As experience builds, training should expand to include other topics such as the following: an overview of unfamiliar subject areas; technical skills, like keyboard shortcuts; chat etiquette; and service guidelines. Additional training issues culled from Miami Libraries chat transcripts indicate that approximately 25% of the questions are not typical reference questions. As a result, staff needed additional training to understand circulation and interlibrary loan policies, general university information, authenticating with a proxy server, and connecting to university servers.

CONCLUSION

Library administrators must not only realize that chat is here to stay, but also that it is just the beginning of a new era of digital reference services. The next few years will see rapid improvements in technologies to provide digital reference. Voice over IP, for example, is the newest Excitement feature, which will eventually become a Basic feature. Traditional reference services are not likely to disappear any time soon, but it is clear that client interest in new digital services is increasing; demand for traditional service will therefore surely decrease in proportion. Although there may be some initial reluctance on the part of staff, it has been the limited experience at Miami that a committed training program and a measured, incremental introduction of chat service can empower staff and create a flexible, quality service. But first, library administrators need to create an environment where the service can flourish Only then will customers experience the Excitement of trying out new digital services such as chat. In turn, the interactions that result and the feedback generated from having customers use and appreciate these new services validate and further empower staff. Finally, the authors believe that a positive first experience with chat reference is crucial. This experience has the power to influence staff response to future concepts of digital reference, and it can remove much of the suspicion and reluctance that attended the introduction of chat. A positive first experience with chat reference can keep libraries agile enough to both anticipate and respond to evolving customer needs.

NOTES

1. Joshua Boyer, "Virtual Reference at North Carolina State: The First One Hundred Days," *Information Technology and Libraries* 20, no. 3 (September 2001): 122-8; Kelly Broughton, "Our Experiment in Online, Real-Time Reference," *Computers in Libraries* 2, no. 4 (April 2001): 26-31; Jo Kibbee, David Ward and Wei Ma, "Virtual Service, Real Data: Results of a Pilot Study," *Reference Services Review* 30, no. 4 (2002): 25-36.

2. R. David Lankes, "Birth Cries of Digital Reference," *Reference & User Services Quarterly* 39, no. 4 (summer 2000): 352-90.

3. Thompson, Jim. *Q.I. Story Team Leader Training.* Cincinnati, Ohio: L.E.A.D. Co.

4. Timothy Butler and James Waldroop, "Job Sculpting," *Harvard Business Review* 77, no. 5 (September/October 1999): 144-153.

5. Rob Casson, "RAKIM Stuff," Available: <http://styro.lib.muohio.edu/rakim/>. Accessed: August 12, 2002.

6. Bernie Sloan, "Ready for Reference: Academic Libraries Offer Live Web-Based Reference, Evaluating System Use," July 11, 2001. Available: http://www.lis.uiuc.edu/~b-sloan/r4r.final.htm. Accessed: August 12, 2002.

Live Reference Chat
from a Customer Service Perspective

Edana McCaffery Cichanowicz

SUMMARY. Suffolk Cooperative Library System has been constructing a digital reference infrastructure predicated on the question "How
will this work at the point of service?" In 2000, Suffolk added a live chat
reference service in order to better assist patrons at the digital point of
service. Staffing, hours, and other administrative decisions were tested
against patron needs. This article describes the development process and
discusses software selection and development issues with regard to patron needs. *[Article copies available for a fee from The Haworth Document Delivery Service: 1-800-HAWORTH. E-mail address: <docdelivery@haworthpress.
com> Website: <http://www.HaworthPress.com> © 2003 by The Haworth Press,
Inc. All rights reserved.]*

KEYWORDS. Point of service, collaborative reference systems, real-
time reference, staffing, scheduling, models, Suffolk Cooperative Library System

---

Edana McCaffery Cichanowicz (ecichano@suffolk.lib.ny.us) is Development Co-
ordinator/Reference Services and Emerging Technology, Suffolk Cooperative Library
System, 627 North Sunrise Service Road, Bellport, NY 11713.

[Haworth co-indexing entry note]: "Live Reference Chat from a Customer Service Perspective."
Cichanowicz, Edana McCaffery. Co-published simultaneously in *Internet Reference Services Quarterly* (The
Haworth Information Press, an imprint of The Haworth Press, Inc.) Vol. 8, No. 1/2, 2003, pp. 27-32; and: *Virtual Reference Services: Issues and Trends* (ed: Stacey Kimmel, and Jennifer Heise) The Haworth Information Press, an imprint of The Haworth Press, Inc., 2003, pp. 27-32. Single or multiple copies of this article are
available for a fee from The Haworth Document Delivery Service [1-800-HAWORTH, 9:00 a.m. - 5:00 p.m.
(EST). E-mail address: docdelivery@haworthpress.com].

http://www.haworthpress.com/store/product.asp?sku=J136
© 2003 by The Haworth Press, Inc. All rights reserved.
10.1300/J136v08n01_04

INTRODUCTION

The fifty-five public libraries of the Suffolk Cooperative Library System began constructing a digital reference infrastructure in the mid-1990s. The infrastructure's development followed the evolution of the Internet, from text through graphics, from collecting "free" Web sites for library home pages to establishing a Web-based digital collection. The most radical feature of the project, however, may be its insistence on conforming technology to a customer service standard, not vice versa. Suffolk Cooperative Library System's vision was to dovetail a core reference collection with existing resources, train staff in all the member libraries to most effectively use it, and provide technical support as the need arose, realizing that all three elements, collection, training and technical support, work synergistically to create a successful customer service outcome. Digital resources were never viewed as peripheral to real reference, but as integral parts of a changing information culture, central to the continued vitality of reference at the point of service.

Suffolk librarians do not define chat as a technology but as a service using a new technology to increase the market penetration of reference into our local communities. They see it as a mechanism to achieve greater customer satisfaction by desktop delivery of information. Management decisions are relentlessly predicated on the question, "How will this work at the point of service?" or more ambitiously, "Where does this fail at the point of service?" with full knowledge that the latter has become a moving target.

Heretofore the point of service has most often been synchronous contact, either at the reference desk or via telephone, between the patron and librarian. Success is dependent on the ability of the parties to collaborate in a reference interview, leading to a complete answer to the patron's question, and with immediate provision of the answer as the most desirable outcome, from a customer service standpoint. Live chat presents all the challenges of face-to-face or telephone reference, but the point of service has become virtual. The reference librarian becomes an agent operating within the patron's desktop environment. Librarians are performing their traditional role, but in a radical new dimension.

This article is descriptive (and not necessarily prescriptive) of one large suburban consortium's experience in beginning to move from a static digital reference collection to an interactive digital reference service via the implementation of a live chat component.

STAFFING

No administrator is likely to seriously propose that purchasing, cataloging and shelving materials is the totality of reference; that the possession of a physical collection is synonymous with service. A print collection without a professional reference staff to provide assistance and guidance is a ludicrous concept. Likewise, to consider a digital collection, without the interactivity which can be provided by human reference librarians, as the totality of digital reference service would be equally misguided.

By early 2000 the Suffolk Cooperative Library System realized that the Virtual Reference Collection <http://vrc.suffolk.lib.ny.us> had become unwieldy for patrons, if not for reference librarians. Staff suspected that customers, faced with such a large collection of resources, would "give up" and go to Google or Yahoo!, rather than attempt to navigate databases into which we had invested considerable time and money. One response to the cluttered environment certainly would be to ratchet up the service to include online help, as retailers such as Land's End and QVC were doing in order to transact their core business online.

Colleagues in academic libraries were already running live chat services, many of them using free software. Based on limited funding, Suffolk librarians decided that by creatively reassigning staff and using free software, they could launch a pilot project to assess public library patrons' readiness to engage in interactive digital reference.

The project has grown from Sunday Night Live, a 7 hours per week after hours service which went online on September 10, 2000, to the robust 38 hours per week Live Librarian service <http://www.suffolk.lib.ny.us/snl/>. Since inception, there has been e-mail back-up to integrate chat into the reference department at each of the fifty-five member libraries. When the service is "offline," patrons may leave an e-mail reference question which is, in most cases, referred back to the patron's home library. Thus, the core collection previously housed in a central physical location has been decentralized onto each accessible desktop, and the central reference process has grown to include a referral-back function, rather than only a referral-up (in difficulty of question posed) function.

Library administrators frequently ask if staffing a live chat service could be done by library school students, with the desperation of the questioner inversely proportional to the amount of anticipated funding for the project. This question is based on a view of live chat reference as being an add-on, something extra, not part of the real reference department. Librarians would think twice before exploiting library school students as reference librarian volunteers in the bricks and mortar building. Why would live chat be viewed differently?

If, however, libraries confront the staffing issue with the question, "How can we effectively increase the market penetration of the reference staff? In what service areas are we consistently failing, and at what hours?" they are more likely to arrive at a staffing outcome which will be judged satisfactory, at the point of service, by the customer, the librarian and ultimately the administration.

In practical terms this means that libraries may not immediately jump into a 24/7 totally live chat scenario. Nor do they need to. Statistics demonstrate that while Suffolk patrons have some use of the digital collection during the middle of the night, the vast majority of use occurs from about 9:00 a.m. to 9:00 or 10:00 p.m. EST. Just as the reference desks in library buildings are staffed based on real traffic, librarians should at least consider staffing our virtual desks at their correspondingly high traffic times. Suffolk patron's high traffic period for database usage is from the traditional beginning of the workday, through the time of evening when most people are packing it in for the night. Why would librarians assume that hordes of people are waiting to ask us questions at 4:00 a.m.?

Experience has borne this out. Our pilot project, Sunday Night Live, offered live chat from 5:00 p.m. to midnight on Sunday nights, at a time when staff anticipated that patrons were trying to get last-minute homework help. The service was virtually unused between 11:00 p.m. and midnight. Suffolk librarians now close the Live Librarian service at 11:00 p.m., offering extended hours, but refraining from striving to impose 24/7 as a Platonic ideal.

Of far more practical importance than 24/7 is the demonstrable need for multilingual staff. While Suffolk Library System would be hard pressed to install foreign-language-speaking librarians in each of the 61 buildings, perhaps the need for such service can be addressed at a virtual focal point. The first group of virtual librarians possesses excellent reading and writing abilities in English, Spanish, German and Russian. An important recruitment goal is to build on this foundation. While the Live Librarian service does not yet have enough multilingual librarians to offer scheduled assistance in each of the languages for which there is a growing local demand, staff hopes to launch a Spanish language service component by January 2003.

Another frequently asked question is "Can live chat be performed at the reference desk?" Suffolk Library System has chosen not to. The main argument against doing so is that face-to-face patrons may perceive the chatting librarian as ignoring them. So while it is tempting to assign live chat out at the desk, to save money in staffing, it's potentially a problem vis-à-vis the patrons' perception of service. Live Librarian staff plan to experiment with one late-night shift in August, to test whether live chat at the desk is feasible at an adequately staffed desk, late on a weeknight during school vacation.

SOFTWARE CONSIDERATIONS

From the customer viewpoint, what is absolutely essential in live chat software? Before selecting a product, it's a good idea to visit a Web site using that product to offer customer support. This preliminary scouting foray can be, but need not be, to a library chat site. Play with asking questions and get a feel for the process from the customer's end. If you are considering co-browsing, try this feature via a dial-in connection, if that's what your patrons will be using. You may discover co-browsing to be too sluggish to use in actual practice.

The easiest scenario for the patron is to avoid software requiring special downloads or plug-ins. Otherwise, one must supply technical support for the plug-in. Simply clicking on the link for chat should open the session, presenting the patron with a simple log in procedure.

If the service is not staffed 24/7, and you intend to accept offline e-mail questions, what information do you need in order to answer the e-mail? Because Live Librarian staff refer these queries back to the respective member library within the consortium, the system needs to collect a home library and/or zip code. Depending upon your online hours, a hybridized chat/e-mail service may generate less chat and more e-mail than you anticipate during the initial planning stage. Either is capable of achieving direct desktop delivery of the answer, each is interdependent.

The most compelling feature of chat, from the patrons' viewpoint, seems to be the ability to receive pushed pages. This feature is comparable to a librarian opening a book and handing it to a patron, and often better, in terms of delivery, than telephone reference. Communication and document delivery are both achieved via one instrument, within the desktop environment. An electronic document is easier for many patrons to manage than a photocopy or print object. They have the bibliographic information as part of the document, they can manipulate the text, they can cut and paste quotes. If preferable, nothing has to be re-keyed.

From the librarians' viewpoint, the ability to send canned responses is vital, lest the transaction become a typing test. When you implement the system, keep the pre-set responses simple. Include "Does this completely answer your question?" as part of terminating the process.

PRODUCT DEVELOPMENT AND VENDOR RELATIONS

Suffolk Libraries' subscription databases are IP authenticated. Some of them quite reliably "push" onto the patron's desktop through the virtual reference software. Others do not. This is an area where vendors can and must work with librarians to assure maximum flexibility. Currently, many online database vendors' technical support staff have no idea what a page pushing problem is.

The missing other half of interactive digital reference is the metasearch tool. This will enable both patrons and librarians to more efficiently search across multiple databases. One can easily imagine a scenario where a patron's failed search automatically routes to the chat librarian, as sort of a digital reference intensive care routine. Experienced librarians have all seen the visibly agitated patron, engaged in a seemingly fruitless search, and approached with a smiling "Are you finding what you're looking for?" Live chat could become a comparable digital intervention, although the courtesies need to be decided. Could the preferred level at which intervention occurs be part of a barcode log-in, like a patron-type? As in, "this patron wishes to try independently until s/he initiates request for live help."

CONCLUSION

When not hyper-identified as primarily a new form of information technology, the live chat model can serve to build and maintain customer relations. It can bring meaningful interactivity to an increasingly chaotic online environment. It can brand the library as a provider of personalized information delivery. It can establish the library as the local storefront on what we used to call the information superhighway. Much as a local broadcaster or cable station reaches into the local household, the library has the ability to penetrate markets at this level, becoming the public broadcasting segment of the Internet spectrum.

Staffing a Real-Time Reference Service: The University of Florida Experience

Jana Smith Ronan

SUMMARY. Librarians are exploring a variety of models to staff new chat-based reference services in an effort to better serve users outside of the library. This article explores the issues in staffing a reference service operating in real-time. Observations are based on the experience of the author in administrating *RefeXpress*, the real-time reference service at the University of Florida, and on a survey of practices in other library settings. The issues addressed include service hours, staff competencies, scheduling, structuring the work environment, and choosing a centralized versus a decentralized model of operation. *[Article copies available for a fee from The Haworth Document Delivery Service: 1-800-HAWORTH. E-mail address: <docdelivery@haworthpress.com> Website: <http://www.HaworthPress.com> © 2003 by The Haworth Press, Inc. All rights reserved.]*

KEYWORDS. Virtual reference service, staffing, University of Florida, chat reference, models, administration

INTRODUCTION

Public, academic, and other types of libraries are adding reference assistance in real-time, often called chat reference, to their bevy of online services

Jana Smith Ronan (jronan@ufl.edu) is Interactive Reference Coordinator, George A. Smathers Libraries, POB 117001, University of Florida, Gainesville, FL 32611.

[Haworth co-indexing entry note]: "Staffing a Real-Time Reference Service: The University of Florida Experience." Ronan, Jana Smith. Co-published simultaneously in *Internet Reference Services Quarterly* (The Haworth Information Press, an imprint of The Haworth Press, Inc.) Vol. 8, No. 1/2, 2003, pp. 33-47; and: *Virtual Reference Services: Issues and Trends* (ed: Stacey Kimmel, and Jennifer Heise) The Haworth Information Press, an imprint of The Haworth Press, Inc., 2003, pp. 33-47. Single or multiple copies of this article are available for a fee from The Haworth Document Delivery Service [1-800-HAWORTH, 9:00 a.m. - 5:00 p.m. (EST). E-mail address: docdelivery@haworthpress.com].

http://www.haworthpress.com/store/product.asp?sku=J136
© 2003 by The Haworth Press, Inc. All rights reserved.
10.1300/J136v08n01_05

at an exponential rate. In the rush to add chat and other real-time technology to reference services, it is easy to let software selection and other computer-related aspects of the project dominate planning. However, it is crucial to consider the human side of the service–the people who will be answering the questions. Users connect to chat reference when they encounter a problem and need the intervention of a knowledgeable person. As librarian Anne Marie Parsons puts it, "Regardless of whether a user is interacting with an unseen human miles away or standing before the reference desk, the sense of connection to another being is an important part of the reference experience."[1] A library can spend thousands of dollars purchasing software and promoting online assistance in real-time, but when it comes to user satisfaction, a virtual reference service such as real-time chat or e-mail is only as effective as the person at the other end answering the questions. There are many issues involved in staffing an effective real-time reference service. This article touches upon a few of these issues, including user expectations and staff competencies, service hours, scheduling, structuring the work environment, and choosing a centralized versus a decentralized model of operation.

STAFF ROLES

There are several staff roles involved in the development and operation of a real-time reference service: the planners; the staff members that work directly with users answering questions; the coordinator who tends to daily operations; and the project manager or administrator that oversees the entire operation (as adapted from the McClennan and Memmott model of digital reference).[2] Depending upon the size and complexity of the operation, sometimes these roles are combined or divided across positions. In small libraries or systems, the planning, coordination, administration, and even reference functions may be carried out by one librarian, while in a larger environment such as a consortium or a library with several branch libraries, these responsibilities may be divided among several people. At the George A. Smathers Libraries of the University of Florida (UF), *RefeXpress* is powered by a sophisticated suite of software called NetAgent. NetAgent is often deployed in commercial Web-based call centers and is now being marketed directly to libraries as the Virtual Reference Desk™ from divine, inc. *RefeXpress* staff members consist of an information technology coordinator who oversees software, server, or networking issues; a service coordinator; an assistant service coordinator, a planning team made up of librarians from various units; and last but not least, more than thirty librarians and staff who work with users. The interactive reference planning team sets policy and procedures and advises on training, hours of service, publicity, and future plans. The coordinators manage the day-to-day operations of the service such as scheduling and training staff, maintaining the chat Web site, providing statistical reports, and other routine duties.

Another example is the Q and A NJ project <http://www.qandanj.org>, a real-time reference cooperative of more than thirty libraries in New Jersey that is hosted by Library Systems and Services, LLC (LSSI). A central project manager coordinates the service, working with project managers at member libraries who assist in day-to-day operations such as recruiting, scheduling, and supervising staff. Yet another level of administration operates at LSSI to handle question overflow and outsourced hours. Coordinating an online real-time reference service is a topic deserving of an article unto itself; the remainder of this article focuses on the staff in direct contact with library users.

MEETING USER EXPECTATIONS

Users have very high expectations for online assistance. While some users may be initially impressed by flashy features such as escorting (guided assistance through a series of Web pages) or white boarding (an electronic shared workspace or drawing board), the importance of these features pale in comparison to the level of service received from the person on duty. Users won't return for help a second time if the person answering the question is unhelpful, unresponsive, or slow in responding to queries. The longer the time where there is a lack of feedback such as a greeting, status report, or new Web page to look at, the more likely it is that the user will experience frustration or even disconnect from the service.

Librarians can learn from the business world, where many Web-based call centers answer consumer questions under the assumption that the average consumer will wait 90-120 seconds.[3] E-commerce call centers on the Web use benchmarking and develop formulas such as the ubiquitous "80/20" industry standard[4] to determine the amount of time a consumer need wait to talk to a representative. Adherents of the 80/20 standard require call center workers to respond to 80% of the incoming calls within twenty seconds. This is not to advocate libraries adopt such benchmarks or rules. Reference transactions are usually much too complex or varied to apply rules formulated for settings where most answers can rapidly be delivered from pages from one Web site. These commercial standards are valuable to librarians as they give an indication of the length of time an online user will wait for assistance before abandoning the session. Online reference staff can strive to greet users within 90-120 seconds at the very least, start negotiating to get at the user's true need, and then give the user an estimate for the time involved in finding an answer.

To provide users with timely, personalized assistance, it is important to select staff based upon certain competencies, or to train librarians to master these real-time reference skills.

REAL-TIME REFERENCE COMPETENCIES

Education

What are the characteristics or competencies of an effective real-time reference worker? Certainly knowledge of online reference sources ranging from proprietary databases to search engines is very important, but what about education or computer skills? Some librarians feel very strongly that only trained professionals possessing an MLS or similar level of education should staff a library chat service, as is the case with Ask a Librarian, the real-time reference service of the Santa Monica Public Library.[5] Others feel that with training, library school students and support staff members are well suited to triage or even to answer questions. The libraries at University of Illinois at Champaign-Urbana Libraries <http://www.library.uiuc.edu/ugl/vr/> and the University of South Florida <http://www.lib.usf.edu/virtual/services/index.html> both employ library school students to work with users in their chat services.[6] At UF, librarians staffed *RefeXpress* the first year of operation, but later the staffing model was extended to include library assistants. This decision was made after an analysis of chat transcripts revealed that many questions were of the same type routinely handled by support staff at in-house reference desks. For example, a large volume of questions involved verifying bibliographic citations, locating online databases, and advising undergraduates on resources for beginning research. Library assistants now work with users in *RefeXpress* but are scheduled at times when librarians are available to step in and assist with research level questions.

Some chat reference services even outsource certain kinds of questions to outside experts such as online homework tutors or specialists outside the field of librarianship. For example, through the CLEVNET Library Consortium's KnowItNow 24X7 service <http://www.cpl.org/vrd/learnmore.html>, users can consult with registered nurses working for the Cleveland MetroHealth Line.[7] KnowItNow 24X7 also contracts with commercial vendor Tutor.com to provide children assistance with schoolwork.

Computer Skills

While there is no real consensus among real-time reference practitioners on the level of library education needed to staff a chat reference service, other competencies are more clear-cut. Most readers will agree that computer skills such as typing, familiarity with Windows-like applications, and multi-tasking are essential for working as a chat librarian.[8] UF staff members discovered that many chat users become impatient when working with slow typists, and some even log off before getting a full answer to their question. (Slow typists may find it more effective to respond to questions via e-mail.) The ability to multi-task, or work with more than one program or Web browser window at a time, reduces the amount of time taken to find an answer. Librarians who can multi-task will be more productive as they can read e-mail, write reports, and work on other tasks while waiting for calls from users.

Another important computer skill is chatting, or instant messaging. Recruiting staff with experience in chatting and other synchronous online communication may be hard if one is limited to the existing reference desk ranks. Janes' recent survey of 648 public and academic librarians revealed that 68.2% of the respondents had never tried instant messaging, while 65% had never chatted.[9] This survey indicates that in 2001, the majority of the librarians working in the field lacked experience chatting. One would suspect that with the recent surge in interest, the number of librarians without chat experience would be on the decline. Lack of experience does not disqualify a librarian from consideration; if a librarian is comfortable with computers and possesses the other competencies listed below, chatting is relatively easy to learn.

Desired Competencies for Chat Reference Staff

In summary, an effective online chat librarian possesses the following skills or interpersonal attributes:

- Good reference interviewing and communication skills
- Familiarity with reference sources, especially online resources such as library databases, directories of Internet resources, and search engines
- Ability to improvise and think creatively
- Knowledge of referral procedures, whether referring users to the reference desk, another library, or a face-to-face consultation with a librarian or subject specialist
- Ability to type fairly quickly
- High comfort level with computers and networking
- A willingness to learn
- Ability to express oneself in writing
- Experience in synchronous online communication such as chatting or instant messaging

Most of these skills are part of an accomplished reference librarian's repertoire. Other skills, such as conducting an effective reference transaction online, typically require training and practice before librarians feel comfortable working alone online. Once the desired competencies have been identified, the issue of staffing resources/availability becomes the primary concern.

RECRUITING PERSONNEL

Staffing a real-time reference service is a simple matter for an institution with a generous budget. In this scenario, coordinators find it easy to lure talented online reference librarians to work for generous salaries. There might even be a budget line to outfit a virtual reference center with high-speed networking and computers, new office furniture and an additional core reference collection. Staff would vie to cover late night and weekend hours for overtime, enabling coordinators to schedule services twenty-four hours a day, seven days a week. Unfortunately chat services seeking to operate within an existing reference budget may find personnel issues challenging. A new service may have to contend with competing reference priorities or reductions in budgets. Realistically speaking, staffing and recruitment tends to be one of the more problematic areas in getting a fledgling real-time reference service up and running. Many online live reference services debut with modest service hours and a small number of staff.

Personnel selection is critical to the success of an online live reference service, and it is important to think this through carefully. The choice of staff will almost certainly impact the hours of service, scheduling, the work environment, and many other administrative aspects of the service. Several questions should be considered in decision-making. What competencies are realistic to require of real-time reference staff, given the pool of personnel to draw upon? Which skills will staff acquire via training? Will staffing be limited to professionals possessing a degree in library science? Does the library budget support hiring new librarians or other personnel? Will subject specialists be recruited in addition to reference generalists? What if librarians are not available for staffing after 5 p.m.? If support personnel are to be included, will adding chat to their duties necessitate adding more hours to their work week and create an overtime pay situation? If so, are there union limitations on working more than forty hours a week? For libraries with already overburdened public services staff, would banding together in a shared service with other departments, branches, or libraries make sense? These are just a few of the questions to consider when selecting personnel.

Some Staffing Strategies

Once core competencies for chat reference workers have been established, there are a variety of ways to accomplish the actual staffing. New staff can be hired, existing reference staff can be reassigned, or volunteers can be recruited. Outsourcing late night hours or even the complete chat operation to a local consortium or commercial service, such as the Metropolitan Cooperative Library System's 24/7 Reference or LSSI, may also be an option. A few libraries have created new positions to administer and staff new chat services, while others have recruited existing personnel to work additional hours for extra pay. Two large public library consortia, the NOLA Regional Library System of Ohio[10] and the Suffolk Cooperative Library System of New York state,[11] recruit staff from member libraries as independent reference contractors to cover evening chat hours. Late night real-time reference personnel are paid an hourly wage above and beyond their regular library salaries. However, two models seem to dominate in academic libraries: recruiting volunteers from existing reference staff, or adjusting librarians' reference duties to incorporate virtual reference desk hours. For example, the library administration at The State University of New York (SUNY) Buffalo recruits librarians to contribute one hour a week to staff Instant Librarian.[12] At UF, public service reference librarians are required to work two hours a week in *RefeXpress*, in addition to other regularly assigned reference and library instruction duties.

The Pilot as a Recruiting Tool

Library managers considering whether to start a real-time reference service may find that staff members are reluctant to participate. In this situation, it may be possible to recruit a small team of volunteers to test chat reference in a pilot program or trial. During the pilot, staff become familiar with reference in real-time as they observe volunteers working with online users. This can help allay any fears or reservations about the value of online assistance via chat, especially if user response is positive. A test run also aids the library's planning team in identifying challenges for full-scale implementation, such as finding people to work late at night. In addition, a successful pilot can lead to administrative (and staff) support to either hire new positions or incorporate chat duties into existing job descriptions.

THE WORK ENVIRONMENT

There are a variety of ways to structure the work environment of an online real-time reference service. Some libraries employ a centralized model where every staff member is physically situated in one location, such as the reference desk or a room stocked with ready reference books, scanners, computers, and telephones. Other online real-time reference services are more decentralized, and librarians work anywhere they wish provided they have a networked computer. The location of the service will also depend on whether the staff member will provide other public services at the same time, such as e-mail reference, information desk, or reference desk duties.

Centralization

At the Auburn University Libraries, the InfoChat service operates using a centralized organizational model. Shortly before Auburn began its real-time reference service, the four subject area reference desks were consolidated into "one centralized reference services desk in the main library," and chat software was installed "at one of four computer terminals at that centralized service point."[13] As many as four librarians, staff, and graduate students work at this desk, but no fewer than two are available at all times to answer chat, telephone and walk-in questions. Another example of a centralized model is the chat service of the North Carolina State University (NCSU) Libraries. At NCSU, telephone, e-mail, and real-time questions are handled in an off-site services desk equipped with computers and extra phone directories and schedules. This desk is located near the reference desk and collections.[14]

Using a central location as a base of chat operations has certain advantages. If everyone works in one location, it eliminates the need to duplicate and maintain client software, computer hardware, and peripherals such as scanners in numerous locations. Print reference sources can be made available by physically situating chat workers near the reference collection, or by establishing a chat center in one location stocked with directories, encyclopedias, style guides, and other ready reference tools. The centralized chat operation is also more convenient to manage in several ways. Locating staff in one room, or at one desk, ensures that librarians see each other when changing shifts and can pass on news of technical glitches or "hot questions." Centralization also makes it possible to fold chat scheduling into the existing reference desk or telephone reference services operations. This is a popular model for staffing large commercial call centers where chat, e-mail, and voice over Internet protocol (VoIP) transactions number in the thousands a week, as it is easier to administer and keep workers productive.

However, situating a real-time service at a reference desk has certain disadvantages. At the reference desk staff members are frequently away from the desk and can't hear the chat bell ringing or see a remote user connect for help. In addition, on busy days librarians may face continual interruptions from in-house patrons. This can result in less than optimal service for remote users. A centralized staffing model may also make it difficult to recruit librarians and staff to work certain hours if they must work at the designated chat reference area. Giving staff the latitude to work out of their offices or to telecommute from home helps "sweeten" those late night or rush hour reference shifts. For example, most *RefeXpress* librarians covering the 5 p.m. to 9 p.m. shifts choose to work from home, often using a library-owned laptop computer.

Distributed Staffing

The most flexible of models for librarians, coordinators, and project managers alike, decentralized staffing seems to be the most popular across all library types. In this type of organization, librarians may work from a variety of locations: in the same library building; in branch libraries on the same campus or across a city; or across several counties, cities, states, and even countries. For example, at UF, librarians from eight branch libraries work out of their offices and homes. On rare occasions, when short of staff, staff members also work at the reference desk. Ready for Reference, the real-time reference service of the Alliance Library System in Illinois is another example. The Ready for Reference service is composed of eight Illinois college and university libraries. Each library covers the service approximately eight hours a week, and the remaining weekend and late night hours are outsourced to LSSI.[15] Some libraries make use of time zones when staffing their services. The Boeing Company's Ask a Librarian service opens with the librarians at the St. Louis location in the morning, and then moves to librarians in Arizona, California, and Puget Sound as the day progresses.[16]

Probably the chief advantage of staffing in a decentralized manner is the flexibility to tap into expertise and staff from a variety of locations. This model enables a library to cooperate with other libraries or systems and share a chat reference service–an attractive option for smaller libraries. For staff, an important advantage is the latitude to work in an environment where they know the layout and feel comfortable.

Working with personnel distributed across a variety of locales does raise certain challenges, especially in coordinating personnel and procedures. Managing a decentralized service demands more effort to keep up with staff, especially when there is a complicated schedule of staff working from a variety of locales and even different organizations. It's important that the chat coordinator set up special communication channels and schedules for staff, as well as clear procedures for covering vacations, shift trades, and absences due to sick time, forgetting a shift, or tardiness. At UF, staff members are scheduled to work *RefeXpress* for a semester at a time; the staff schedule is posted on the

Web for easy access. A Microsoft Outlook-generated dynamic calendar is used to track shift trades on a day-to-day basis. *RefeXpress* participants discuss issues and ideas, post announcements, and make requests to trade shifts using an internal e-mail address list in Microsoft Outlook. Staff also telephone and instant message each other during shifts if they need help.

COMBINING CHAT AND IN-HOUSE REFERENCE

Is it a good idea to base a chat out of a reference desk? There are definitely pros and cons to working with remote and walk-in clientele at the same service point. Many real-time reference services do operate from a traditional reference desk, such as Ask A Librarian Live at Austin Peay State University[17] and TalkNow at Temple University.[18] Some librarians prefer to base chat services at the reference desk because of convenience of scheduling, proximity to collections and the built-in backup from other staff. For others, a blending of the two services may be a compromise because a lack of personnel makes it difficult to offer a real-time reference service separately from the reference desk.

Basing a real-time reference service at a reference desk raises certain operational questions. For example, who takes the online chat questions when librarians are also fielding questions from users on the phone or walking up to the reference desk? Will any staff member be open to chat, or will one be specifically assigned to take chat users? How will the person chatting handle walk-in visitors? How will chat-based questions be handled at desks structured around tiered or differentiated service models, or where librarians are encouraged to rove? What are the priorities in answering in-house, telephone, and chat users? How does scheduling work when librarians from several branches or libraries at different locations are logged on? These are just a few of the policy issues that may need to be clarified so as to provide effective service.

Chat at the Traditional Reference Desk

Several libraries base their chat services at the reference desk, and it's helpful to examine how this works in practice. At the University of Illinois Champaign-Urbana Libraries, chat questions come to one reference desk, and the answering responsibilities can fall to any of the three staff members working at the desk at that time.[19] The person that is free takes the question from the remote user. Other services designate one person to field online questions, while her or his coworkers focus on in-house users. In other libraries, several librarians may be logged on to take questions at the same time. At Temple, "staff from several different libraries can log onto TalkNow simultaneously," which increases "the odds that when one desk is busy, another has staff available to answer a particular question."[20] This is the most decentralized of all staffing approaches.

Chatting Away from the Reference Desk

Many libraries have experimented with locating chat librarians at the reference desk, only to move chatting to offices or other non-reference desk locations. Why? "Communicating in a virtual environment is labor intensive," according to Antonelli and Tarlton.[21] Librarians report that the environment at the reference desk is too boisterous to concentrate when working with online users. Often during a chat reference transaction, the librarian jumps from conducting a reference interview, to searching in databases to find answers, then finally, sending or pushing information to a user. It is very intense, especially for the librarian just learning to chat or attempting to master a sophisticated new software program. In addition, it is easy to become frustrated and distracted due to interruptions from nearby in-house users or colleagues. SUNY Buffalo moved chat away from the reference desk because librarians found working at the desk under this arrangement too distracting, and because their software (AOL Instant Messenger) gave no user logon cues. Also, the software did not notify online visitors that librarians were busy if the librarians happened to be away from the desk.[22]

Librarians using sophisticated software seem to have more success in combining traditional and chat services. This is due in large part, no doubt, to features such as automated responses that alert users when the librarian is occupied and sound or visual cues that alert librarians to incoming calls. At UF, for example, NetAgent generates a popup window and a repeating chime that sounds until the librarian responds to a new logon. The librarian also hears a chime each time the user posts a new comment. Such alerts allow the librarian to multi-task while staying aware of users. Yet, even when chat software includes such cues, it is difficult for librarians to concentrate on an online user when an in-house user is demanding attention or the phone is ringing. This is one reason why UF does not normally schedule *RefeXpress* shifts in conjunction with shifts at the libraries' reference desks.

Perhaps the Lippincott Library of the Wharton School at the University of Pennsylvania <http://www.library.upenn.edu/lippincott/RefDeskLive/> has achieved a balance in the debate whether to chat or not to chat at the reference desk. Librarians at Lippincott cover some chat hours at their reference desk, but chat services are moved to a quieter locale during busy hours.[23] Some libraries may find it necessary to base chat service at the reference desk, but it is likely that working in an office or a separate chat reference center ensures that distance users receive the same level of service as in-house users.

GENERAL SERVICE OR SUBJECT EXPERTISE SERVICE

Staffing a virtual reference desk does offer flexibility in how librarians are presented to online users. Software can be configured to set up a general help desk and single starting point, or users may be allowed to select a librarian based on subject knowledge or expertise. With the general approach, all users are routed through one entry point, and users don't know who will be answering their questions. For example, when users log on to *RefeXpress*, the software connects them to a librarian that happens to be on duty that hour. Other libraries have their logons set up so that users select a librarian based upon subject expertise or availability. For example, users of RefChat at the Gutman Library of the University of Philadelphia <http://www.philau.edu/library/refchat.htm> see a directory of RefChat librarians when they log on, including subject background and their online hours. The user can choose to initiate a chat with whoever happens to be online, or return later to work with a particular librarian. At CLEVNET's KnowItNow 24X7, users are presented with a variety of subject areas when logging on. If they select the general reference option, they are routed to the main question queue in the software where generalists work with users. When users select "science," their questions are either fed to or drawn from the queue by the science librarian.

STAFF IMPACT ON SERVICE HOURS

The way in which a service is peopled has a tremendous impact upon hours of availability, particularly with a new service. There are three basic factors that come into play. These factors are: the number of staff and their hours of availability; volumes of questions; and the feasibility of extending hours via outsourcing or shared staffing across institutional lines.

Setting Service Hours

When setting service hours, one should first identify patterns of user activity, and then compare the hours to staff availability. Look for hours of highest user activity–when users are accessing the library's Web site and online databases, e-mailing reference questions, or visiting the reference desk. After user patterns are identified, strive to cover hours when usage is the highest, followed by hours of moderate activity. Incidentally, online usage at UF closely parallels in-house reference desk use, peaking between the hours of 11:00 a.m. to 2:00 p.m. during the week. The goal is to establish a "core" of chat reference hours that staff can cover; hours can expand as the service matures.

What if there are not adequate personnel to cover peak user hours of activity? Start small and work to expand coverage over time–up to 24/7 coverage if that is the goal. Begin by establishing real-time reference service during regular reference desk hours. The Library of Congress <http://www.loc.gov/rr/askalib/> is piloting real-time reference one hour a day on weekdays. The public libraries of Suffolk County, NY, ran a pilot project (Sunday Night Live) on Sunday evenings for three months before committing to a more extensive service schedule.[24] It's common for libraries to start with service hours as low as ten hours a week, as did the Libraries at Vanderbilt University <http://www.library.vanderbilt.edu/heard/librarian.shtml>, and to progressively work up to broader hours of service over several semesters or months of operation. Ask a Librarian Live at Vanderbilt moved to twenty hours a week after one semester.[25] UF staffed the pilot of *RefeXpress* twenty hours a week with six volunteers, but now offers services fifty-six hours a week during the school year.

Sharing and Outsourcing Hours

A shortage of staff may be an impetus for joining a cooperative, where hours can be divided among staff at several libraries and staff in different time zones can cover late night hours. UF is exploring collaboration with other research libraries in Florida and the Association of Southeastern Research Libraries (ASERL). The goal of this collaboration is to extend weeknight hours after 9:00 p.m. and add weekend coverage. Other options include contracting with a library vendor to cover problematic hours such as late nights and weekends, or completely outsourcing the real-time reference service, budget permitting.

Matching Demand

Large libraries and/or shared services with a heavy volume of chat traffic may find it challenging to match staff to the number of chat questions. Some software helps manage situations like this by allowing staff to work with more than one user at a time. An extra librarian can be scheduled on call to handle unanticipated "spikes" in volume. Another option is to route questions to a library vendor's reference center for assistance when a service is overwhelmed by users. Both LSSI and 24/7 Reference offer a service with professional librarians to handle calls.

CONCLUSION

One of the most critical points in operating an online real-time reference operation is that of staffing. Staffing a service at this particular juncture in time can be challenging because real-time communication technology is unfamiliar to so many practicing librarians (and professional staff).[26] Each library seeking to offer online reference assistance via real-time technology will bring a distinct (and often finite) mix of human and financial resources to such a project. Happily, there are a variety of ways to establish service hours, staffing and other personnel matters, regardless of the resources at hand.

NOTES

1. Anne Marie Parsons, "Digital Reference: How Libraries Can Compete with Aska Services," *Digital Library Federation (DLF) Newsletter* 2, no.1 (January 2001). Available: <http://www.diglib.org/pubs/news02_01/>. Accessed: August 1, 2002.

2. Michael McClennan and Patricia Memmott, "Roles in Digital Reference," *Information Technology & Libraries*, 20. September 2001. Available: <http://www.lita.org/ital/2003_mcclennan.html/>. Accessed: April 24, 2002.

3. Call center industry metrics, or standards for timely response to customers, are discussed in the following articles: Ety Zohar, Avishai Mandelbaum, Nahum Shimkin, "Adaptive Behavior of Impatient Customers in Tele-Queues: Theory and Empirical Support," *Management Science* 48, no. 4 (April 2002): 566-583; Teri Robinson, "The Customer Service Clicking Clock," *CRMDaily.com*, May 7, 2002. Available: <http://www.crmdaily.com/perl/story/17621.html>. Accessed: September 10, 2002; and Pamela Trickey and Penny Reynolds, "From Call Center Agent to Net Rep: Web-Enabling Your Front-Line Staff," *Customer Interaction Solutions*, February 2002. Available: <http://www.tmcnet.com/cis/0202/0202cccms.htm>. Accessed: September 10, 2002.

4. Bill Hall and Jon Anton, "Optimize Your Call Center Through Simulation," *Customer Interaction Solutions*, September 1998. Available: <http://www.tmcnet.com/articles/ccsmag/0998/feature04.html>. Accessed: September 10, 2002.

5. Sally J. Jacobs, "[DIG-REF] 24/7 'Live Person' Service." *DIG_REF Listserv*. Message No. 3576, May 18, 2001. Available: <http://www.vrd.org/Dig_Ref/dig_ref.shtml>. Accessed: May 19, 2001.

6. Carol Ann Borchert, "Virtual Reference Service at the University of South Florida: A Case Study," in *Online Reference in Real-Time*, ed. by J. Ronan (Englewood, CO: Libraries Unlimited, in press); and Jo Kibbee, David Ward and Wei Ma, "Virtual Service, Real Data: Results of a Pilot Study," *Reference Services Review* 30, no.1 (2002): 25-36.

7. The MetroHealth System, *MetroHealth Online Tour*. (Cleveland, OH: 2002). Available: <http://www.metrohealth.org/tour/page12.asp>. Accessed: April 24, 2002.

8. Michelle Fiander, "Re: [DIG_REF] Pre-employment Testing," *DIG_REF Listserv*. December 15, 2001. Available: <http://www.vrd.org/Dig_Ref/dig_ref.shtml>. Accessed: December 16, 2001.

9. Joseph Janes, "Digital Reference: Reference Librarians' Experiences and Attitudes." *Journal of the American Society for Information Science and Technology* 53, no.7 (2002): 549-566.

10. Norman Oder, "The Shape of E-Reference." *Library Journal*, February 1, 2001, 46-50.

11. Tara J. Hoag and Edana McCaffery Cichanowicz, "Going Prime Time with Live Chat Reference," *Computers in Libraries* 21, no.8 (September 2001): 40-4.

12. Marianne Foley, "Instant Messaging Reference in an Academic Library: A Case Study," *College & Research Libraries* 63, no.1 (2002): 36-45.

13. JoAnn Sears, "Chat Reference Service: An Analysis of One Semester's Data," *Issues in Science and Technology Librarianship* 32 (Fall 2001). Available: <http://www.istl.org/istl/01-fall/article2.html>. Accessed: April 11, 2002.

14. Eric Anderson, Josh Boyer, and Karen Ciccone, "Remote Reference Services at the North Carolina State University Libraries," in *Facets of Digital Reference: Proceedings from The Virtual Reference Desk 2nd Annual Digital Reference Conference*, Seattle, WA, 2000. Available: <http://www.vrd.org/conferences/VRD2000/proceedings/boyer-anderson-ciccone12-14.shtml>. Accessed: January 16, 2002.

15. Bernie Sloan, *Evaluating System Use*. July 11, 2001. Available: <http://alexia.lis.uiuc.edu/~b-sloan/r4r.final.htm>. Accessed: July 19, 2002.

16. Julie Martin, "Ask A Librarian Service" (paper presented at *Setting Standards and Making it Real*, 3rd Annual Virtual Reference Desk Conference, Orlando, FL: 2001). Available: <http://www.vrd.org/conferences/VRD2001/proceedings/jmartin.shtml>. Accessed: March 27, 2002.

17. DeAnne Luck, "Austin Peay State University–Ask A Librarian: A Case Study" in *Online Reference in Real-Time*, ed. by J. Ronan (Englewood, CO: Libraries Unlimited, in press).

18. Sam Stormont, "Interactive Reference Project–Assessment After Two Years," in *Facets of Digital Reference: Proceedings from The Virtual Reference Desk 2nd Annual Digital Reference Conference*, Seattle, WA, 2000. Available: <http://www.vrd.org/conferences/VRD2000/proceedings/stormont.shtml>. Accessed January 31, 2002.

19. Jo Kibbee, David Ward and Wei Ma, "Virtual Service, Real Data: Results of a Pilot Study." *Reference Services Review* 30, no.1 (2002): 25-36.

20. Foley.

21. Monika J. Antonelli and Martha Tarlton, "The University of North Texas Libraries' Online Reference Help Desk," in *Digital Reference Service in the New Millennium* (New York: Neal-Schuman, 2000).

22. Hoag and Cichanowicz.

23. Linda Eichler and Michael Halperin, "LivePerson: Keeping Reference Alive and Clicking," *EContent* 23, no.3 (2000): 63-6.

24. Hoag and Cichanowicz.

25. Katherine Porter, "Re: [DIG_REF] Scheduling Chat Services," *DIG_REF Listserv*. April 30, 2002. Available: <http://www.vrd.org/Dig_Ref/dig_ref.shtml>. Accessed: May 1, 2002.

26. Janes.

Q and A NJ:
Service Design and Impact

Marianne F. Sweet
David M. Lisa
Dale E. Colston

SUMMARY. Q and A NJ is a virtual reference service provided by multitype libraries across the state of New Jersey. This article describes Q and A NJ's development and organization and points out elements of both that account for the project's success. The article also enumerates how the project has impacted its participating libraries and their users. Libraries looking to adopt virtual reference should be left with several take away points on what to consider when planning and implementing a virtual reference service. *[Article copies available for a fee from The Haworth Document Delivery Service: 1-800-HAWORTH. E-mail address: <docdelivery@ haworthpress.com> Website: <http://www.HaworthPress.com> © 2003 by The Haworth Press, Inc. All rights reserved.]*

KEYWORDS. Virtual reference, New Jersey, libraries, impact, project management, regional library cooperatives, Library Services and Technology Act (LSTA)

Marianne F. Sweet (marianne_sweet@yahoo.com) is Project Coordinator for Q and A NJ, a statewide Virtual Reference Service in New Jersey. David M. Lisa (davidlisa@ davidlisa.com) is Reference Librarian and Webmaster, Wayne Public Library, Wayne, NJ. Dale E. Colston (dcolston@npl.org) is Reference Librarian, Business, Science and Technology Reference Center, Newark Public Library.

[Haworth co-indexing entry note]: "Q and A NJ: Service Design and Impact." Sweet, Marianne F., David M. Lisa, and Dale E. Colston. Co-published simultaneously in *Internet Reference Services Quarterly* (The Haworth Information Press, an imprint of The Haworth Press, Inc.) Vol. 8, No. 1/2, 2003, pp. 49-69; and: *Virtual Reference Services: Issues and Trends* (ed: Stacey Kimmel, and Jennifer Heise) The Haworth Information Press, an imprint of The Haworth Press, Inc., 2003, pp. 49-69. Single or multiple copies of this article are available for a fee from The Haworth Document Delivery Service [1-800-HAWORTH, 9:00 a.m. - 5:00 p.m. (EST). E-mail address: docdelivery@haworthpress.com].

INTRODUCTION

Q and A NJ[1] was conceived when the libraries of the South Jersey Regional Cooperative (SJRLC) charged their Executive Director, Karen Hyman, to develop a new service that would raise their profiles within their communities. They were seeking the cutting edge–something that would test their comfort level. Two years later, Q and A NJ, now a flourishing service provided for New Jersey state residents by thirty-three libraries and information services statewide, has produced the desired results. It has developed new skills and competencies among its staffing librarians and exercised existing know-how in a new environment. It has proved that virtual reference, as far as the public is concerned, is a service whose time has come. Always available (24/7), Q and A NJ averages 2,500 sessions a month.

How did Q and A NJ arrive here less than one year after opening shop? This article describes Q and A NJ's development and how the service has impacted two of its participants, Newark Public Library and Wayne Public Library, their staff, and their users.

PROJECT TIMELINE

Spring 2000

Select SJRLC libraries agreed to adopt a high profile service, funded by SJRLC.

Fall 2000

The libraries decided on virtual reference and began meeting with different vendors of Web-based reference software. Library Systems and Services Incorporated's (LSSI) virtual reference software was selected.[2] (See <http://www.lssi.com> for more information.)

Winter 2000/2001

Q and A NJ's ten original participating libraries began training on the software. While predominantly public library staffed, the project was multitype from the beginning, with the Burlington and Gloucester County Colleges and the University of Medicine and Dentistry of New Jersey, Stratford Campus, fielding general reference questions.

Spring 2001

Before going "live," the participants decided to team up with libraries from the Central Jersey Regional Library Cooperative (CJRLC) in order to expand the service's capabilities, especially hours of service and reach. Nine libraries from CJRLC were recruited.

Going statewide also meant that the project was eligible for federal Library Services and Technology Act (LSTA) funding, through the New Jersey State Library.

Norma Blake, New Jersey State Librarian, said "Let's make it statewide!" and SJRLC was thrilled to oblige.

SJRLC administered the project, which was funded for one year. The objective was to "assist public librarians to provide a real-time, interactive Web-based, ready-reference service that enables reference librarians to assist patrons in remote locations to find the information that they need."

Grant funds could be used for LSSI costs for simultaneous librarian logins, or seats, installation, and training; project staff; public relations and publicity, including a custom Web site; and LSSI service fees. SJRLC purchased a fourth seat from LSSI, dedicated to a question queue monitored by the Educational Information and Resource Center (EIRC).

Summer 2001

While training and practicing continued among participating libraries, SJRLC contracted with a graphic designer to create artwork–logo, Web graphics, banner ad, poster, bookmark, and sticker designs–for what was now called Q and A NJ.

A full-time Project Coordinator/Analyst with both library and Web management backgrounds was hired. The project coordinator created a Customer Entry Web site <http://www.qandanj.org> and a project Web site <http://www.qandanj.org/manual>. (See Appendix, Figures 3 and 4.)

Fall 2001

On October 1, Q and A NJ was officially launched.

Nineteen libraries and information services staffed the service forty-four hours per week: 1:00 to 11:00 p.m. Monday through Thursday and 1:00 to 5:00 p.m. on Friday. New Jersey Nightline, New Jersey's after-hours toll-free reference service at the East Brunswick Public Library, provided staffing between 9:00 and 11:00 p.m.

Two weeks before the official launch date, the service was "soft launched"–i.e., the service went live without prior publicity except for word of mouth to colleagues, families, and friends of participating librarians. The first press release announcing Q and A NJ went out on the same day to newspapers local to participating libraries.

SJRLC held a second recruitment round in order to move the project northwards–to attract more participating libraries in the northern half of the state–and to enable the service to expand its hours, possibly to 24/7. Seven libraries from the Central Jersey, INFOLINK, and Highlands Regional Library Cooperatives signed up. All four of New Jersey's regional library cooperatives were now on Q and A NJ's roster.

The Project Coordinator took over training responsibilities from LSSI. With these training costs saved, the project was able to outsource overnight and weekend coverage of Q and A NJ to LSSI's Web Reference Center.

Winter 2001/2002

On January 28, 2002, Q and A NJ went 24/7. Participating libraries expanded their coverage to between 9:00 a.m. and 11:00 p.m. Monday through Thursday and between 9:00 a.m. and 5:00 p.m. on Friday. LSSI provided coverage for the remainder of the time, i.e., overnight and weekends. A second round of press releases coincided with the new hours and new geographical representation by participating libraries. A flurry of media coverage resulted, and usage surged 500% in the first week of new hours, a level at which usage eventually stabilized.

In order to fill in a few shortages on the virtual reference desk, SJRLC made its most recent recruitment pitch to libraries statewide. Libraries with annual budgets of around or more than $1 million were approached. Seven libraries signed up to join the others in March and April 2002. (A list of participating libraries can be found at <http://www.qandanj.org/about.htm>.)

Spring 2002

With its success in attracting participating libraries, users, and the media, Q and A NJ was able to obtain a second, larger LSTA grant. Q and A NJ is currently funded by the New Jersey State Library with LSTA dollars through April 2003.

PROJECT STRUCTURE AND MANAGEMENT

In exchange for staffing the virtual reference desk six hours per week, Q and A NJ participating libraries have the entire cost of start-up, training, and software for shared use of LSSI's Virtual Reference Toolkit covered by the project. There is no special software required for participants, so their investment is purely one of staff time.

Each library also designates a Project Manager, who meets once a month with fellow Project Managers to share and respond to new and emerging issues. Meetings inevitably give rise to new group norms and thereby foster a shared understanding of what the service is all about–its ideals, goals, and practices. A boon to the project, New Jersey's small size makes these face-to-face meetings possible.

More than two hundred experienced adult reference and youth services librarians from 33 participating libraries and information services statewide staff Q and A NJ. In such a large distributed environment, communication is key to successful collaboration. The structure for communication among project participants consists of the monthly library project managers meetings; two private online discussion groups (one open to all staffing librarians and one to library project managers only); a project Web site; and the Project Coordinator. In addition, training brings project members together initially. It provides an opportunity for librarians from different libraries and different parts of the state to meet each other, and for service policies to be communicated.

The full-time project coordinator's role is to facilitate all these communication channels. She is point person for both library project managers and staffing librarians. She divides her time among troubleshooting, service guidance, creating support materials, ensuring substitutes are found,[3] meeting preparation, Web site maintenance, training, transcript/data analysis, and direct provision of the virtual reference service.

The project Web site at <http://www.qandanj.org/manual> is common ground for librarians from disparate libraries. There they find software instructions, competency checklists, service guidelines, staff and library information, virtual reference tools created specifically for the project, meeting minutes, and other material.

CUSTOMER PROFILES

Q and A NJ customers are probably representative of the patrons of participating libraries. An analysis of reference session transcripts reveals that approximately 30% of service users are students. Personal information, openly provided through a customer feedback survey, reveals a diverse user base. For example, occupations range from Environmental Protection Specialist to school bus driver. Nearly a third of Q and A NJ customers complete the survey, which automatically launches when a reference session ends. Table 1 presents a profile of Q and A NJ customers, based on a sample of survey respondents.

MARKETING

Most users heard about Q and A NJ by word of mouth, while surfing the Internet or from a search engine, at school, and on their library's Web site.

All participating libraries pitch in to get the word out about Q and A NJ. Some of their activities include distributing bookmarks to local bookstores and other storefront outlets (Borders and Barnes & Noble are enthusiastic distributors); distributing bookmarks and posters to local schools and government; presenting Q and A NJ at conferences and special programs; and contacting local media about Q and A NJ.

Public relations professionals from East Brunswick and Somerset County Libraries drafted model press releases that were widely adapted by SJRLC and participating libraries.

Since Q and A NJ is actively promoted by its participating libraries, many of its customers are probably also participating libraries' patrons. A statistical analysis of customer zip codes supports this.

Probably the three most successful marketing decisions made by the project were to design a banner ad that is a call to action and encourage participating libraries to prominently place the ad on their Web site (see appendix, Figure 5); to aggressively promote Q and A NJ to New Jersey teachers and schools, a definite affinity market; and to expand hours to 24/7.

CHARACTERISTICS OF THE SERVICE

Questions Submitted

As with Q and A NJ customers, questions submitted to the service are probably similar to those posed by the patrons of participating libraries. Although

TABLE 1. Customer Profiles (Percentage of Respondents)

Gender		Age			
Male	Female	1 to 18	19 to 35	36 to 59	60 and up
34%	66%	27%	18%	44%	11%

Data collected from the third week in January-April 2002.

the project was initially conceived as a ready-reference service, the questions actually submitted are a lot more diverse, ranging from in-depth research to library-specific questions. Figure 1 shows some sample questions.

Q and A NJ is fortunate because all the of its participating libraries have access to the same journal article databases from EBSCOhost, and most have a few other proprietary databases in common. Because of this overlapping resource base, participants feel their library patrons receive relatively the same service from another library. At the same time, since information can usually be found in more than one resource (print and electronic), access to the same resources has proved less important than providing consistent, high quality service.

Customer feedback is overwhelmingly positive. When asked what they liked about the experience, customers most often mention five attributes of the service: the interaction with a live person; they got the answer or the librarian was helpful; the service is always open; the library came to them; and the service is fast. These attributes are precisely the benefits that Q and NJ and virtual reference, in general, are designed to bring their users.

Call Statistics

What is it like on the virtual reference desk? The following snapshot of Q and A NJ call traffic means to provide a quantitative introduction.

An average of three librarians from separate libraries staff the virtual reference desk at any time. Librarians who started at the beginning of the project have seen the average number of sessions they each handle per hour (between

FIGURE 1

SAMPLE QUESTIONS

- What was the most significant event during the 1850s in bringing about the Civil War?
- I am looking for information in preparing homemade treats for my pets (dog and cat).
- We are looking for a diagram of a football stadium (not the field) to create a model (grade 6).
- I want to locate a new energy supplier which offers lower rates for gas.
- Where can I find a list of descriptions of each character in the musical "Carousel"?
- I need the township codes for an in-ground pool for Wayne, NJ.
- Can I use WebCat for an interlibrary loan? If so, how?

9 a.m. and 9 p.m. weekdays) triple, from approximately two calls in October 2001 to approximately six calls in May 2002. The total sessions handled per month by Q and A NJ grew approximately 600% between opening day and the last month of the school year, May 2002. Table 2 gives month-by-month totals.

As Table 2 shows, call traffic grew exponentially, almost literally overnight, during the first week that Q and A NJ went 24/7. While weekend hours account for 50% of that growth, most of the remaining growth occurred not in the overnight hours but between 9:00 a.m. and 11:00 p.m. "Always open" seemed to attract new users to the service and not necessary during overnight hours.

Q and A NJ's busiest times are between noon and 3:00 p.m. on weekdays and during varying time-blocks between 2:00 and 8:00 p.m. on weekends. Busiest days are Monday, Tuesday, and Wednesday.

The average session duration is 10 to 15 minutes with notable statistical clusters in the 20 to 25 minute range, though it is not unusual for sessions to last 40 to 45 minutes. Since libraries cover the virtual reference desk in two-hour slots, a staffing librarian typically will handle four calls during her or his two-hour shift.

IMPACT ON PARTICIPATING LIBRARIES

Newark Public Library[4] and Wayne Public Library[5] joined Q and A NJ respectively in November 2001 and February 2002. Although Q and A NJ is in a relatively early stage, these libraries' experiences, echoed by the more veteran project participants, can shed light on the potential impact of virtual reference on the library as an institution, and on the library's staff and users.

Local versus "Global"

The first point is that when Newark Public Library and Wayne Public Library librarians are on the virtual reference desk they serve a broader community than their own. It is uncertain whom they will be serving, but most of the time it is someone from another library's community.

TABLE 2. Q and A NJ Monthly Call Totals, 2001-2002

Oct '01	Nov	Dec	Jan '02	Feb	March	April	May	June
451	415	479	813	2,265	2,484	2,593	2,568	1,354

Sometimes it is very apparent that they are providing reference to a state-wide audience, especially when a customer asks about a topic that is specific to a location unfamiliar to the librarian or is not reflected in that library's collection. Yet this new element is just another manifestation of how the Internet is changing reference services and affecting libraries. Since the Internet is here to stay, participating in Q and A NJ is a necessary part of conducting reference services.

Q and A NJ customers understand the benefit of their libraries' participation. Customers who need reference services during hours and days which their libraries are not open and those who are "on the go" express great interest and gratitude that they can get answers on a Sunday evening, for example, via Q and A NJ. (Q and A NJ is promoted as another way to submit reference questions not only outside of, but also during, the library's operating hours.)

Policy Conflict

Potentially, policies at participating libraries can conflict with project-wide policies for handling different situations stemming from types of questions, customer behavior, transaction length, etc. Both Newark and Wayne libraries work under the assumption that participation in Q and A NJ brings its own set of guidelines. Instead of conflicts, what participating librarians have found is a strong agreement on procedures.

For example, according to The Newark Public Library Reference Service Policy, the library "shall seek to provide users with complete, accurate answers to their information queries regardless of the complexity of those queries," a level of service that is mirrored by Q and A NJ.

Q and A NJ equates chat-based reference to telephone reference, which provided participating librarians a set of guidelines that they were already familiar with. Accordingly, participants aim to answer Q and A NJ questions in a smaller time frame than onsite reference questions. Librarians will continue to work on questions after the online session ends, but extensive research falls outside of the parameters of both the local libraries and Q and A NJ.

Perhaps transaction time poses the greatest difference between the way things are done at the physical reference desk and the virtual reference desk. Q and A NJ is designed to "provide fast answers to questions using information found on the Internet and in proprietary databases funded by libraries." (See home page.) This means that while Q and A NJ librarians may take as long as necessary to answer a question, the service's resources–namely the supply of librarians vis-à-vis a greater number of customers on hold–often place a limit on the amount of time a librarian can spend with a Q and A NJ customer. Q and A NJ's Web site prepares users for fifteen minutes or less with a librarian, who will answer the question or get the customer started if the question involves lengthy research. This situational time constraint can be stressful to librarians at first. Both Wayne and Newark librarians have adapted to enforcing shorter transaction times on Q and A NJ.

Q and A NJ also differs in the choice of resources used to answer the question. Choosing to use the Internet and proprietary databases over print resources is not just a stylistic difference (between the "electronic librarian" and the print-oriented librarian). The virtual reference software interface is designed to push Web pages to users. Therefore, librarians must be willing and able to use and point customers to digital sources of information to effectively use the software.

Skills Involved

Since virtual reference is conducted through a Web-based interface, Q and A NJ librarians at the very least must know how to operate a Web browser. The virtual reference software requires working with and between multiple windows, so librarians must also be proficient in window management. Experience with chat software like AOL Instant Messenger or ICQ is helpful to reduce the technological learning curve.

Wayne Public Library staff has found that being familiar with PCs and software operation in general is an advantage because it is certain that some time or another something will go wrong during virtual sessions–either on the librarian's side or the customer's. Librarians may be called upon to recover from a browser freezing up or the operating system crashing; to troubleshoot a hardware problem; or to diagnose an interrupted Internet connection. (Likewise, more up-to-date technology reduces the chance of software and hardware problems. Fortunately, because Newark and Wayne Public libraries had an adequate level of technology in place at the outset, joining Q and A NJ did not require additional expenditure in this area.) Virtual reference is not immune to the vulnerabilities of other Internet- and computer-based work. Librarians must act fast to correct the situation before the customer is lost.

Both Newark and Wayne librarians were proficient in online searching and using Microsoft Windows® prior to joining Q and A NJ. Though none of our librarians were familiar with virtual reference software, the above computing skills set significantly prepared them for Q and A NJ.

Ease of Communication

Virtual reference is all about telling, not showing. Without non-verbal cues and physical movement (including the material world of the library), librarians in a virtual reference session use only text, or verbal communication, to conduct a thorough reference interview and to point out where and how the information is found. Also, users bring to this environment varying degrees of communication skills, from unfamiliarity with chat to poor grammar and spelling to inadequately describing the research problem. There are many reasons why it is critical that virtual reference librarians become skilled in chat-based communication.

Since virtual reference interaction is limited to text, participating librarians have found that clarification of the question is the most important and the most necessary part of the virtual reference transaction. For example, Q and A NJ customers often pose partial questions, as if entering keywords in a search engine. A customer who submits "breast cancer" as their question could be asking for a variety of things: a definition of the disease, statistics, courses of treatment, periodical articles, and so on. Moreover, without further probing the information need, how would the librarian know that we are providing information appropriate to the customer's age? The customer could be a middle school student doing a science fair project or someone inquiring on behalf of his afflicted wife.

When chatting with a customer, virtual reference librarians must also make a concerted effort to keep the session alive and interactive by maintaining contact with the customer, who has less cues about the librarian's activities than the librarian has of the customer's. This may mean the librarian sending a status message every couple of minutes during the course of executing a search strategy. Continuously moving back and forth between chat and searching is the virtual reference librarian's standard technique. And at the end of the session, it is especially important to ensure that the customer is pleased with the results. Otherwise, closure can be difficult to accomplish.

Finally, the virtual reference librarian must become an adept communicator who can overcome interfering technical difficulties. Internet connection problems, unequal Internet access speeds, the distraction of recovering from software problems, etc., can add confusion to the interaction between the librarian and customer. For example, the librarian may push a Web page that takes longer to load up on the customer's side or even freezes that customer's browser. The librarian must be alert to this possibility when interpreting the customer's response, or non-response, to the librarian's actions.

Finding the Answer

Q and A NJ's provides an answer to approximately 86% of questions handled by the service. Q and A NJ defines a completely answered question as one that the librarian has answered to his or her satisfaction and includes referrals in this category. (Customers sometimes disconnect before acknowledging that the information does answer the question.)

Reference librarians would like to deliver each answer quickly, concisely, and tailored to each patron. However, some answers are not forthcoming in a reasonable amount of time, especially given Q and A NJ's particular environment. What is a "reasonable" amount of time can be determined by the customer, e.g., the amount of time the customer is able to remain on the line, and by the librarian, e.g., the amount of time the librarian can spend with an individual customer when there are other customers on hold or when the librarian reaches a "point of diminishing returns" (when further searching will not produce more or better results).

When the answer cannot be found or found in a reasonable amount of time, our staffing librarians generally have three options. The librarian could choose to work on the question at a later time and contact the customer when the question is answered. If the librarian determines that she or he will not be able to locate the answer (using available resources), she or he could forward the question to New Jersey's statewide reference center at the Camden County Library, which is designated to take questions of this type. Lastly, the librarian could suggest that another Q and A NJ librarian take a look at the question, and then transfer the session back into the question queue or to a particular librarian on virtual duty. Usually, any of these choices serve to eventually provide the answer.

Of course, some customers' urgency prevents the librarian from providing an adequate and thorough search of available resources, so their questions remain unanswered. Fortunately, Newark Public and Wayne Public librarians are very familiar with the Internet and other resources. Their overall experience has been that finding the answer or getting customers started on a fruitful course of research is seldom a problem.

The digital environment in which virtual librarians work facilitates providing value-added service. The role of the reference librarian is to evaluate and interpret information, not just to deliver it. Not only do librarians perform this role on Q and A NJ–the service's very selling point–they also package or format answers for customers. For example, when appropriate they gather information and data from multiple sources into word processing or spreadsheet files. Aggregating the information makes it more comprehensible. They also download articles from periodical databases (usually in HTML or PDF format) and other types of online information and send them to the customer using the virtual reference software's file sharing capability. This gives customers content that they would not have access to on their own, including, for some, through their local library.

Types of Questions

Users' differing expectations of what Q and A NJ can do for them results in a variety of types of questions submitted to Q and A NJ. Most questions are standard to traditional reference service. We've encountered five major question categories: facts, analysis/synthesis, opinions or advice, homework, and library-specific information.

Factual questions include, for example, requests for biographical data, company directory information, and facts about states and countries. "What is the history of the National Teacher's Exam?" and "What does HVAC stand for?" are factual questions fielded by Newark. Many factual questions are not ready-reference and may be time-consuming to answer. Sources have to be evaluated by librarians and some answers are not readily found using online resources. Faxing pages and mailing photocopied pages from print collections are occasional ways to get the answer to Q and A NJ customers.

"I need to prepare for a debate. What educational system is better? The United States or France?" illustrates an analysis/synthesis question. These types of questions can be complicated and require too much time to research in an online reference session. Online resources may also be inadequate to answer them. We usually handle analysis/synthesis questions by making sure customers understand the research assignment and its requirements and by providing sources of information to get them started. These questions can also present the perfect opportunity to refer customers to their local library.

In response to opinions or advice questions, such as "Should the medication Remeron® be taken with Aricept®?" we provide sources of information, instead of a definitive answer.

Homework questions, such as requests to complete a multiple choice or a true-false questionnaire or to answer a chemistry or math problem, are approached the same way as opinion questions. Typically the librarian leads the customer to where they will find the answer or instruction.

Because the Q and A NJ banner ad is placed on participating libraries' Web sites, some users assume they have reached a service of their local library. They are looking for answers to the fifth type of question, such as how to place holds or renew overdue library materials. Handling this type of question has become standard to the Q and A NJ service. If librarians can answer the question using the other library's online resources, such as its Web site or online catalog, then they will. However, Q and A NJ librarians never paraphrase other libraries' policies that are unclear to them. Instead they refer the customer back to the local library.

The sheer variety of questions can challenge the virtual reference librarian, who may not have had the opportunity to field such a mix at the Q and A NJ participating library. A youth services librarian who fields questions from adults for most of her or his Q and A NJ shift, may feel especially gratified when she or he finally pickups a customer asking a question in her or his specialization, such as a request to recommend books for a 10-year-old girl. After a while, all Q and A NJ librarians become generalists and their knowledge of Internet resources grows exponentially.

Handling Customers

Like customers at the physical reference desks, the type of customers served during any given Q and A NJ shift partly depends upon situational factors such as time of day, relationship to the academic year, occurrence of significant current events, school assignments, etc.

From children completing homework assignments to seniors looking for health care information, from the casual Internet surfer looking for recipes to professionals seeking statistical data, Q and A NJ customers make for new experiences in every shift at the virtual reference desk.

Variety is a good thing, variety being what attracted us to libraries, but user makeup can become lopsided during a shift. When that happens, it can be problematic for the service. For example, Q and A NJ has been an unexpected host several times to a whole class of students, who simultaneously log on in their school's computer lab. Apparently, the students have entered the lab en masse after being given a class assignment. To triage this situation librarians trade online the URLs of Web sites they gave to the students. Q and A NJ requests that schools schedule any full classroom sessions in advance.

Different customers bring different attitudes to their interaction with the librarian. Students often connect during school and hurry us up for the answer before their next class period starts–say, in five minutes! In some cases, librarians try to find the answer in that time frame. If unsuccessful, they communicate that another method may be necessary to answer the question (hopefully correcting the students' misunderstanding of the research involved).

Q and A NJ librarians must also be prepared to handle occasional unfriendly or even abusive customers. One of the most challenging customer attitudes is impatience expressed in impolite language. Most of the time librarians are successful at ignoring this behavior and earnestly provide the answer. Less often, there are prank callers with rude or sexually explicit comments.[6]

Scripted messages come to the aid of librarians in these situations as well as in other uncomfortable situations, such as having to tell a user they cannot be served because they are from out of state. Scripted messages, importantly, are a consistent way to handle inappropriate behavior and to enforce certain project-wide policies.

The following two (system-wide) "courtesy" messages are often used together, as a two-stage approach to handling customers whose behavior or language is inappropriate. The librarian sends the first message and gives the customer ample opportunity to desist. The second message alerts the uncooperative customer of the librarian's actions.

- "I will respond to your question as soon as possible. Thank you for your patience."
- "The language you are using is inappropriate. I am disconnecting."

Librarians recognize that the anonymity of the Internet has its advantages and disadvantages. Participating librarians expect and accept occasional uncivil behavior from users of Q and A NJ. They are even aware that some of this seemingly uncivil behavior may simply be chat evolving a more abrupt way of communicating among its frequent users. Q and A NJ participants especially appreciate the service's position in providing answers to questions users may be uncomfortable asking anywhere else. Consequently, staff try to keep an open mind and always give customers the benefit of a doubt, until it is clear that their question or intention is not legitimate. The "prank" question is treated as if it was a "real" question. Doing so ensures that the user's intent has not been misjudged. Not responding in the way the prank caller hopes for discourages many of them.

The vast majority of customers are appreciative, cooperative, and civil. Newark and Wayne Public Library librarians vie to staff the virtual reference desk. However, other prospective virtual reference services and librarians should come equipped to deal with a greater range of customer behavior.

Other Time-Management Issues

Q and A NJ has introduced to participating libraries surmountable staffing and scheduling issues that, nevertheless, are important to emphasize.

Newark and Wayne libraries each provide virtual reference coverage six hours per week. Newark has seven librarians[7] and Wayne has eight librarians who share staffing responsibility. Even with these many trained Q and A NJ librarians, rearranging schedules and assigned duties to accommodate participation in the project was a challenge. While the libraries did not find it necessary to entirely eliminate other services in order to take on virtual reference, some libraries may have to make the trade off.

It has been found necessary to cover the virtual reference desk away from the reference department's physical desk to avoid distractions and interruptions. (Virtual reference requires more concentration than in-person reference.) Libraries looking into providing virtual reference should consider dedicating a remote workstation to the provision of virtual reference, at least during coverage time.

Much as participants feel that Q and A NJ is simply an expansion of our reference services, at times participation is not seamless. This situation particularly arises at the end of a Q and A NJ shift, when librarians must step out of their virtual reference role and return to duties at the participating library. (The exception is librarians who provide coverage from home or who can stay past their assigned shift.) Toward the end of their shift, librarians must quickly steer an in-progress reference session toward a mutual resolution. The transition between roles is somewhat analogous to closing time at the library, but probably is experienced more often by virtual reference librarians.

Of course, if librarians are engaged in sessions that will last beyond their shifts, there are a number of choices they can make about how to dispose the session. If this occurs at the end of day (at the library's closing time), the session can be placed back into the question queue for the (outsourced) overnight librarians to pick up. If it happens in the middle of the day, the librarian can transfer the session directly to a librarian from the next shift. The librarian alerts the customer before essentially handing off their question. Another possibility is that the librarian asks if they can get back to the customer at a later time with the answer, usually via e-mail. Often the customer, having received enough information to get started, prefers no further work on the question.

CONCLUSION

From a project management perspective, Q and A NJ owes its success to the uniform commitment and cooperation of its participating libraries; to the even distribution of responsibility among its participants; to its multiple communication channels, including monthly meetings and a full-time project coordinator position; to its statewide reach which established a critical mass of providers and users as well of publicity; and to being open for business when users are on the Internet–24/7.

Participating libraries have encountered and successfully dealt with numerous issues introduced by participation in Q and A NJ. We conclude this article from an operational perspective, with a list of take away points intended for prospective virtual reference services. The following points summarize the issues we encountered, and their impact on Q and A NJ libraries, staff, and users:

Point 1: In a collaborative virtual reference arrangement, expect to answer or field questions outside of the familiar. Over time, librarians will become generalists and will enhance their reference knowledge.

Point 2: There will probably be more agreement than disagreement between your library's policies and project-wide policies. Look to "the real world," i.e., traditional reference practices, for guidance. The main differences that virtual reference librarians should expect are faster transaction times and a heavier reliance on digital resources.

Point 3: Librarians will be called upon to provide some troubleshooting of technical problems. Virtual reference is not immune to the vagaries of Internet and computer performance.

Point 4: Textual communication is the foundation of virtual reference service. Librarians will have to become excellent chat-based communicators. They will employ and polish their reference interview skills, especially to elicit like responses from their customers.

Point 5: The online environment, even with its limitations, offers the same opportunity as onsite reference to completely answer the question or leave the customer satisfied with the transaction. It also offers a new opportunity for value-added service–by facilitating the librarian's interpretation of the information and the packaging of answers.

Point 6: Most staffing librarians may find little difference between questions submitted to the virtual reference desk and to the physical reference desk. All the same, expect to acknowledge and support those librarians who encounter a greater mix of questions–to their disconcertion–than they field at their participating library.

Point 7: Participating in a collaborative project significantly reduces the number of hours a library must carve out for the provision of the virtual reference service. Sharing the load with other libraries more than compensates for staffing and scheduling constraints introduced by adopting the new reference service.

Virtual reference will certainly proliferate. We've seen receptivity among our library patrons and in our state in general to justify offering the service. We hope that New Jersey's experience and our individual libraries' experiences will help other projects better deal with the set of considerations introduced by implementing the service. If other libraries decide to follow Q and A NJ's model, we feel that they will be effectively utilizing the Internet and its resources to provide information to a newly defined group of users.

NOTES

1. Q and A NJ is administered by the South Jersey Regional Library Cooperative, a state tax-funded service of the New Jersey Library Network, and supported by Federal Library Services and Technology Act funds administered by the New Jersey State Library.

2. LSSI's software combines Internet chat with the ability to send Web pages and files directly to the customer's computer. The LSSI product is a hosted solution. See appendix, Figures 1 and 2 for a view of the software the librarian's and customer's perspectives.

3. Requests for substitutes are made by participating libraries over the general discussion group. Usually requests are successful; when a substitute cannot be found the project coordinator requests coverage from LSSI's Web Reference Center.

4. The Newark Public Library (NPL) is New Jersey's largest public library. Newark itself is the state's most populous city and has the largest Latino and African-American populations of any municipality in the state and the largest Portuguese community in the United States. ("Facts About Newark." Available: <http://www.Guide2Newark.com>-Accessed: June 12, 2002.) NPL has made Internet access available since 1992 and has approximately 225 Internet public use computers across nine facilities. Computer classes are offered in English and Spanish.

5. Wayne Public Library is a medium sized public library in suburban Passaic County and is located approximately twenty miles from New York City. Many residents of Wayne commute into New York City for work. There are more than thirty public use Internet computers in the main library. Most of the Microsoft Office suite of programs is installed on these computers.

6. Approximately 0.5% of sessions contain inappropriate language.

7. Newark Public Library has assigned three librarians from the Arts and Humanities center and four librarians from the Business, Science and Technology Center.

APPENDIX

FIGURE 1. Sample Q and A NJ Reference Session from Librarian's Point of View

APPENDIX (continued)

FIGURE 2. The Session from the Customer's Point of View

FIGURE 3. Q and A NJ Home Page with Customer Entry Activated

FIGURE 4. Q and A NJ's Online Manual for Staffing Librarians

 Library Info | Reference | Support | Service Guidelines | Schedule | Staff | Project | Login

Librarian's Online Manual

News and Announcements

08/14/02 Q and A NJ Customer Feedback Posted Online
08/19/02 Elizabeth J. Cronin, from Ocean County Library's Toms River branch, wins the Samuel Swett Green Award for best virtual reference transcript. Read the press release.
08/21/02 Q and A NJ offers Live Homework Help via Tutor.com starting September 15, 2002.
08/22/02 The next Green Award submission deadline is September 20, 2002. Go here for the award checklist and to submit your model transcript.

Participating Libraries Information

FIGURE 5. Q and A NJ Banner Ad

From AskWendt Live to QuestionPoint™: A Chronology of the Development of a Persistently Virtual Reference Product and Service

John Wanserski

SUMMARY. The author describes how library staff members at the Kurt F. Wendt Library at the University of Wisconsin-Madison collaborated with other campus libraries and a technology company, Convey Systems, to develop a feature-rich virtual reference service designed to support the university's extensive and growing digital collections. The project progressed from an idea, to a beta/pilot, and finally to a full-fledged multi-library service. This chronology offers a detailed examination of the challenges, compromises, and successes in developing software to support a new virtual reference service. Issues covered include technical troubleshooting, testing, training, marketing, and integration with existing digital services. *[Article copies available for a fee from The Haworth Document Delivery Service: 1-800-HAWORTH. E-mail address: <docdelivery@haworthpress.com> Website: <http://www.HaworthPress. com> © 2003 by The Haworth Press, Inc. All rights reserved.]*

KEYWORDS. Virtual reference services, voice over IP, software development

---

John Wanserski is Deputy Director, Kurt F. Wendt Library, University of Wisconsin-Madison.

[Haworth co-indexing entry note]: "From AskWendt Live to QuestionPoint™: A Chronology of the Development of a Persistently Virtual Reference Product and Service." Wanserski, John. Co-published simultaneously in *Internet Reference Services Quarterly* (The Haworth Information Press, an imprint of The Haworth Press, Inc.) Vol. 8, No. 1/2, 2003, pp. 71-94; and: *Virtual Reference Services: Issues and Trends* (ed: Stacey Kimmel, and Jennifer Heise) The Haworth Information Press, an imprint of The Haworth Press, Inc., 2003, pp. 71-94. Single or multiple copies of this article are available for a fee from The Haworth Document Delivery Service [1-800-HAWORTH, 9:00 a.m. - 5:00 p.m. (EST). E-mail address: docdelivery@haworthpress.com].

http://www.haworthpress.com/store/product.asp?sku=J136
10.1300/J136v08n01_07

INTRODUCTION

On May 20, 2002 Convey Systems, Inc. announced a partnership with OCLC to provide system and development resources for integrating the OnDemand™ software into QuestionPoint,™ a collaborative reference service developed by OCLC and the Library of Congress. An initial version of the integrated package was demonstrated at the American Library Association (ALA) Conference in Atlanta on June 13-19, 2002. This paper provides a chronology of the development of this live reference product through the partnership of an academic library and an emerging Web technology company that succeeded due to a history of risk-taking, experimentation, problem-solving, professional collaboration, customer support, but most of all, mutual vision.

THE BEGINNING

There are millions of great resources that are not now on the Web, and may never be–resources like all of those books sitting on shelves in our libraries, content in the proprietary databases that libraries subscribe to, and other information including trade-association data, government records, and literally tons of other material that people can't access through search engines.

–Steve Coffman[1]

Steve Coffman, one of the first visionaries and pioneers in live reference services, has expressed the concern that despite the flood of information on the Web, users are not finding what they need. Taking the point of Coffman's quote a step further, what is missing from the World Wide Web of knowledge is human interaction. Many libraries have invested staff, resources, and space to create digital library collections. The archived intellectual content of recorded time is now entering virtual reality spaces. Streaming audio and video are vehicles for putting the preserved artifacts of art, music, theater, and human events on the Web. Whether library users' needs can be met by accessible Web-based content or more inaccessible print resources, they often need a librarian as guide, facilitator, and finder. Librarians are expert finders and, more often than not, can accurately satisfy difficult queries.[2] Librarians need to populate the new frontier of virtual reference services. This is but one narrative of a digital adventure into that unknown frontier.

The Kurt F. Wendt Library holds subject collections in engineering, computer science, statistics, and atmospheric and oceanic sciences and has long been an innovator and test bed of novel service applications for the University of Wisconsin-Madison library system. Tom Murray, the Director of Wendt Library, has guided staff with a service philosophy and vision that pledges to bring information to users' desktops using the most powerful technology available. The Wendt Library vision statement reads, "Wendt will be the information center of choice for our faculty, staff, students, and other customers and thus will contribute to efficient problem-solving and effective education, research and public service." Wendt staff members have pursued this vision, and Wendt was the first UW-Madison campus library to offer electronic services such as e-mail reference, electronic tables of contents, electronic document delivery, e-reserves, and a Web-based new acquisitions list with tables of contents and book cover images.

During the past fiscal year Wendt Library has purchased more science journals, conference proceedings, and monographs in digital format than in print format.[3] Indexing and abstracting databases link users directly to the full text article or paper. Bibliographic management software programs are linked to these databases to give users the ability to import data to their personal knowledge bases. Whenever and wherever they wish, users select from a multitude of output styles for class assignments, laboratory reports, fieldwork, dissertation or professional papers.

Wendt Library users have a multitude of print resources, but these are now coupled with a number of new electronic access points such as tables of contents for monographs, sample page images, and cover images linked through the OPAC. Remote browsing of collections is supplanting the traditional approach of roaming through the stacks–an approach that users hoped would serendipitously lead them to their next intellectual discovery. Increasingly, Wendt Library's OPAC links to thousands of commercial, free, and governmental Web sites. As Stormont and Meola note in their article in *The Reference Librarian*, "Access to an array of sources that differ in terms of accessibility, interface, organization, and content increases the need for interaction, especially when patrons are not physically in the library."[4]

As collections have moved to the Web, reference services have followed. The AskWendt e-mail service was integrated as a regular function at the reference desk years ago, and requests routinely receive a response within the hour. The response time is more critical for Web-based information because "on average, Americans experience 'search rage' if they don't find what they want within twelve minutes."[5] The immediacy of virtual reference is a logical extension of this service philosophy.

EARLY HISTORY

Early in 2000, Wendt Library staff undertook an exploration of options for developing a real-time reference service that could enable librarians to assist patrons with their database searches. A keyword search in the Computer Select database (later named eShaman, a database that eventually folded) produced a list of companies that specialized in call center software used by merchandise catalog companies and other commercial enterprises. Two of the products reviewed were Human Click and LivePerson. A third company, Videogate, advertised a product with application sharing capability.

A call to John Ingraham, the Director of Virtual Reference Projects at Videogate, verified that their product could, indeed, share applications between workstations using an Internet connection. Their software required both parties to use NetMeeting software and the Internet Explorer (IE) browser. The end user was also required to download and configure Videogate software, called the companion. This presented a substantial roadblock to any reference query initiated from the public workstations of Wendt Library, since these stations were configured with the Netscape browser that was the standard for the UW-Madison Libraries' intranet. Although UW Libraries' system personnel were unable to provide IE for public workstations, the software developers at Videogate accepted the challenge to adapt their product to the Netscape environment.

Three months later, Videogate representatives gave the first live demonstration of their customer relations management (CRM) software configured for Netscape. However, the product worked with Netscape under two conditions. One condition was that the end user had to install the Videogate companion software, a process that is similar to installing a browser plugin such as Adobe Acrobat Reader. The other condition was a requirement that Internet Explorer 5.0 had to be installed (but not launched) on both the agent/operator and the end-user PC. In addition, some of the IE environment files, including a few specific IE "dll" files, were required for the Netscape companion to function.

PROOF OF CONCEPT

With the help of the library's computer services technician, the Videogate companion (the customer/end user piece) software was installed on the Wendt conference room PC. To contact the Videogate site, a staff member at Wendt clicked on a blue telephone button in the upper right corner of the Netscape browser window (version 4.5). The button turned red while the call was being placed, and at the same time, an intermediate screen popped up asking the caller to be patient and stating that the call would be answered in the order that it was received. Once the call was answered, the button returned to its blue color and indicated that a click would "end call." Surprisingly, a digital image of the Videogate operator appeared in the top left hand corner of the browser.

That crucial first connection proved that the Videogate software concept was viable. Text chat was effortless. The operator on the Videogate side could enlarge the staff member's box from a three-line capacity to about thirty lines so that scrolling was unnecessary. Once the chat box was enlarged or "undocked," the staff member was able to drag it anywhere around the browser window. It always floated on top of the browser window no matter what screen was viewed or what application was opened. The box was always available for viewing or composing text, and the perimeter of the box flashed occasionally if the operator wanted the staff member's attention or if a response was needed.

What happened next truly appeared to be a magical moment. A new window opened on the screen without any action on the part of the Wendt staff member. The window displayed the Microsoft Windows calculator, and as library staff watched, the Videogate operator performed a simple calculation on the library computer. The numbers appeared one after the other, moved by the invisible hand of the remote operator. Staff members were then jolted from a state of awe by a crackling human voice coming through the computer's speakers. The smiling operator in the digital photo with the invisible hand on the computer now had a voice. At that moment, staff observing the test realized that voice sounds flowing from one direction of the conversation facilitates communication more efficiently than simple text chatting. The operator was verbally answering the typed questions before the enter key was pressed to send the text! Apparently the operator could also view the staff member's browser screen and the text of the questions that were typed.

The software more than satisfied the initial criteria. Staff members were able to communicate through text chat and voice in real-time, view applications from each other's desktop, and even manipulate one another's applications. After the demonstration, the director of Wendt Library agreed to provide funding for six months that allowed the library to work with Videogate to further develop the beta version compatible with Netscape.

THE BETA VERSION

The University of Wisconsin-Madison campus library system consists of more than forty libraries. Innovation is encouraged and typically begins with small scaleable pilot projects initiated at any of these libraries. While Wendt staff members were engaged with Videogate, other librarians at the Steenbock Library (agriculture and life sciences) and Memorial Library (social sciences and humanities) were experimenting with other software applications for live reference. Robert Sessions, reference librarian in the Steenbock Library, was testing Human Click. Steven Frye, reference librarian in the Memorial Library, was exploring the use of various instant messaging systems. In addition, the campus Reference Coordinators' Committee, comprised of a consensus group of seven middle management librarians from the largest campus libraries (now chaired by Eunice Graupner of the Business Library) met regularly to evaluate live reference products. The Committee sponsored a Public Services Forum on Virtual Reference in December 2000 where Human Click and Videogate applications were demonstrated to campus librarians.

For the Videogate demonstration, a colleague at Wendt acted as the librarian/operator and controlled the agent software. The author acted as the end user. After connecting and chatting with the agent, the author was successfully guided through a search in a ProQuest database. This may have been the first instance of a commercially licensed database utilizing application share technology between an end user and librarian over the Web for a reference transaction. Shortly after the live demonstration, the Reference Coordinators Committee met and encouraged those experimenting with the products to begin pilot services as a means to selecting a live reference product that could be used by all campus libraries.

AskWendt Live IMPLEMENTATION

During Spring Break, March 2001, the AskWendt e-mail reference service became AskWendt Live. It is an ironic coincidence that Videogate also changed its name at this time to Convey Systems. Both name changes were representative of a new focus for providing multiple avenues of communication. For the next three months, three graduate student volunteers from the School of Library and Information Science worked on the project to document and develop the rough outline of the libraries' first live reference service using the Convey Systems' product.

Many features of the Convey Systems' software needed to be customized for implementation. Staff members at Wendt composed wording for the three queue screens that served to inform end users about the progress of their call and the hours of service. When no operator was available the queue screen provided information about alternative routes for questions, such as phone and e-mail reference.

Since a script creation and storage function was not yet available, staff members created script files in Notepad for frequently used responses. With Notepad open on the desktop, the operator was able to perform a simple cut and paste function to get the response to the end user's chat box. Staff experimented with various features, determining which ones worked best with a particular end user's connection speed and peripherals. Although text chat worked well over modem connections, the voice over IP function had a choppy sound.

There were a few bugs to work out with the Netscape version, and Convey representatives were responsive to library staff suggestions and needs. Early on, sharing library database screens over a modem was possible; however, the search process degraded or locked up the consoles after the second or third screen was shared between operator and end user. Communication between workstations on the campus network was much smoother. Voice over IP still had some problems, and Convey technicians suggested using the voice function like a walkie-talkie, toggling on and off as needed. This gave only marginal improvement.

From the beginning of the pilot the service, performance was dependent upon the Internet connection with Convey Systems. Every unit of communication moved over the Internet, from the end user at the local PC, to Convey Systems headquarters in Charlotte, NC, and back to the librarian/operator on the other local PC. Wendt staff soon recognized the need to short-circuit this route. Convey technicians suggested that Wendt Library install a piece of software, called a firewall conference manager (FCM), on a local PC. It ran on a separate PC connected to the campus network and controlled the interactions of the caller and operator.

Staff at Wendt continued to customize other features of the product. Wendt Library's Webmaster helped to create digital images of campus library buildings and service points within the library to display when a librarian or operator answered a call. Images of the libraries were created and inserted in Web pages for the digital photo application. The digital photos can be picked from a list to display in the caller's browser toolbar, adding another dimension of information to the reference transaction. This initial experimentation and incubation period provided a timeframe and structure to prepare for the next test of the concept.

COMMITTEE ON INSTITUTIONAL COOPERATION (CIC) LIVE REFERENCE CONFERENCE

The UW-Madison General Library System hosted a Committee on Institutional Cooperation (CIC) or Big Ten virtual reference conference in Madison during the first week of May 2001. Many of the institutions represented were in the early phases of implementing live reference services. Some Illinois libraries had text chat services in place, and Bernie Sloan of University of Illinois gave a report analyzing some of their query statistics.[6] The statistics from his report served as a guide for the hours of service that were established later at the UW-Madison Library System.

The author had intended to give the first demonstration of a live video transaction with the staff of Convey Systems. Staff had thoroughly checked the live connection and had run through the online script with a librarian/operator at Wendt Library. Sometime during the morning program, the Internet connection between Madison and Charlotte went down. Later it was learned that a denial of service attack occurred in the Washington D.C. area that some attributed to international tensions with the Chinese government over a downed U.S. spy plane. Most Web sites in Washington D.C. were also inaccessible. The live presentation was quickly switched to a static slide show of the project. Of course, the connection worked flawlessly when staff tried the live video connection after the session wrapped up. However, only a few librarians from Michigan and Illinois remained to see this.

WINNING OVER LIBRARY ADMINISTRATION

In May 2001, after much discussion, the Reference Coordinators' Committee recommended that the libraries move forward with Convey's OnDemand software suite as the platform for live reference. Convey had the desired features: application sharing and collaboration; the persistent customizable calling button; voice over IP; a statistics package; reasonable cost for our pilot project; and a development staff willing to shape their product for the library market. The last point was crucial because the complexity of the campus library network and organization presented unusual challenges. With more than forty separate campus libraries and reading rooms representing different administrative structures, the library system acts more like a consortium and requires a high degree of consensus to function.

The campus Electronic Library Committee, chaired by the Associate Director for Automation, met in late May to hear the live reference proposal from the Reference Coordinators' Committee. They agreed to the concept in principle, but had three issues that needed to be resolved. First, as a security concern, the full PC desktop could not be available for application sharing. Second, Convey staff needed to ensure a process that allowed two different licensed owners of their software to have their call buttons on the same resource. For instance, if both Purdue and Wisconsin wanted their calling buttons on the same commercial database, Convey would need a method to display the appropriate button for the caller's institution. And third, a simple method needed to be developed for Web updating of new versions of the companion software by end-users. The development team assured the Committee that their concerns would be addressed before rolling the service out to the public.

Members of the Reference Coordinators' Committee organized into working groups for technical issues, training, policy and procedures, and publicity. Steve Daggett from the Library Technology Group was assigned to add his expertise to the technical issues working group. The Group insured the stability of the FCM server, created a test environment, and organized the process for distribution of the end-user software (companion) to public workstations in campus libraries. Meanwhile, Convey staff had worked through a method for registering library resources so the calling button could appear while a user was in the database. Their programming involved identifying the specific domains or URLs where the call button would appear in the end user's browser. The new method insured that end users would see the call button deep within third-party databases where information reaches its highest levels of complexity. This enhancement feature, unique to the Convey software package, is now known as the Persistent Button. The library was free to customize the persistent call button (see Figure 1) so the button became its own advertisement for the new service. The first attempt to name the service was inspired by the astronomer, Carl Sagan. Although the Live Contact name did draw a lot of attention, it did not deliver enough description.

TESTING AND TRAINING

Over the summer of 2001 the working groups organized another Public Service Forum to introduce the campus reference librarians to the software and explain the broad outline of the pilot service to be introduced during the fall semester. Another group of SLIS student volunteers was trained for the AskWendt Live service. The trainees would provide some early evening hours coverage that summer. Several of them later became library project assistants and worked as operators from the College Library (undergraduate) during the late evening hours.

Robert Sessions, a librarian who had tested Human Click software, helped to extensively test the latest OnDemand software releases. He was able to identify a particularly subtle problem with the companion software developed for the Netscape browser. After sharing applications and using the voice over IP features, the sound quality would degrade and application sharing would slow down. Finally the monitor would turn blue and the computer would crash. This issue became more than troublesome because a crucial go/no-go date for the fall semester was rapidly approaching, and reference librarians participating in the service had not yet been trained.

The first training sessions were devoted to ad hoc stress tests of the system. Because of the problem with the companion software mentioned above, it was decided to postpone the scheduled training. The training and technical working groups spent critical summer days grappling with the cause of the problem and subsequent Netscape browser crashes. Convey eventually identified this as a "memory leak" and devoted staff to solve the bug.

Other facets of the project moved forward. The graphical identity of the service continued to be developed by the graphic artist and public relations staff at the library. A new collection of call buttons (see Figure 2) was designed. The design at the time of this writing employs a blue-gray background using a script font and is less obtrusive than the original Live Contact design. The new Live Help button is an animated GIF image that alternates between the service logo and an arrow with the text "click here."

FIGURE 1. UW-Madison Libraries Live Contact Logo

FIGURE 2. UW-Madison Libraries Live Help Logo

The animation concept was the idea of Steven Feyl, Head of Research and Information Services, Pace University, another early adopter and innovator of Convey software. The artwork for the UW-Madison Libraries queue screens was also changed to match the new call button. The developers at Convey resized the screens (see Figure 3) to balance with the text and designed the windows so links could be embedded to back up e-mail and telephone reference services.

It was now late August 2001, and problems with the Netscape version had yet to be resolved. A few test computers were installed with the companion software in some of the campus libraries near the reference desks. Project members awaited another updated version of the companion/agent software suite from Convey. The technical group agreed that the implementation window for the fall semester had been missed, and the group decided to postpone the training and rollout. Stable software that did not need constant tweaking by the developers was needed before the service could be presented to the public. There were still fifty or so volunteer operators to train, and a phased rollout plan was needed to help manage any unforeseen stress areas on staff or software. There were some among the group who were beginning to question the wisdom of continuing with Convey. A conference call was held with the development team at Convey to discuss strategies. They listened to our concerns and dedicated their efforts to this project. A final software version delivery date was mutually agreed upon for mid-December.

STRESS TESTING–
THE MISSED WINDOW FOR FALL SEMESTER 2001

Once the fall deadline passed, staff members were able to spend more time on other infrastructure issues. The library Web network supported only the Netscape browser for all library resources on the public use machines in campus libraries. The Netscape companion required parts of the IE browser to function and these files had to be installed on public workstations. Although the campus was moving toward use of IE on public workstations, the libraries were at least six months away from deploying and supporting IE as the primary browser. Therefore, the Library Technology Group had to hide or remove the IE icon on all 600 public workstations. IE was, however, installed on the office machines for the volunteer librarian operators.

Tim Whitaker, the Convey lead systems engineer for our project, visited Madison in mid-October 2001 to assist with training and coordination of the implementation. He arrived in time to assist with a thorough stress test. With help from library staff, the Convey team was able to identify the cause of some

FIGURE 3. Live Help Queue Screen

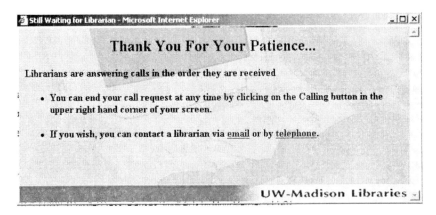

"phantom" calls that had been occurring. When calls from a number of users were placed almost simultaneously, only the last call appeared in the queue of calls on the operator's console. Part of the problem was related to how the Convey computers in Charlotte identified the IP (Internet Protocol) number of the caller PC. Another facet of the problem was related to the built-in time delay used to counteract multiple clicks of the call button. The Convey developers didn't have an immediate solution for the intermittent Netscape crashes previously mentioned, but they installed monitoring software that recorded and transmitted the crash environment to Convey staff. This eventually led to a solution for the memory leak problem noted earlier.

In deploying the companion software on the library network, there were issues aside from hiding the IE icon. The companion software is designed to have new users register their name and e-mail address the first time they use the system. This was problematic because the public workstations always remain online. The first user's registration information would stay in place and, any subsequent users throughout the day could not be identified. Tim and Steve Daggett worked out a solution that enabled new end user registration information to be accepted each time the call button was used on the public workstations.

The visit from the Convey representative was an opportunity to hear about some of the company's future development plans. The representative presented examples of other installations, such as a kiosk installation at Tulsa Public Library, and also demonstrated a statistics reporting package that sites could use to remotely extract transaction data. Convey gained valuable customer relations insights from visits to some of the libraries and computer labs.

ROLLOUT–JANUARY, 2002

During the fall and winter, the public workstations in campus libraries were upgraded to the Windows 2000 operating system (OS), and this became the accepted OS version for the latest upgrade of the OnDemand software suite. Plans were made to distribute future upgrades to the agent software remotely, after this approach was tested by the Library Technology Group. Once staff machines had these upgrades, the Reference Coordinators discussed staffing models and established the project's hours of service.

More than fifty staff from eight campus libraries volunteered to work as operators for the service, including representatives from these areas: Biology, Business, CIMC (education), College (undergraduate), Health Sciences, Memorial (social science/humanities), Steenbock (agriculture), and Wendt (engineering). Each library was free to experiment with whatever service approach worked for them. Most chose to answer calls from their personal offices where they could multi-task during periods of inactivity. Wendt staff worked from an office located near the reference collection. College Library staff answered calls directly from their reference desk. It was eventually agreed to staff the service for forty-five hours a week. There were always two or three librarians as operators at any one time. The hours of service were 1:00 p.m. to 9:00 p.m, Monday to Thursday and 1:00 p.m. to 5:00 p.m. Friday. Later the College Library added some late evening hours: 9:00 p.m. to midnight, Sunday to Tuesday.

The latest agent software (see Figure 4) contains a scripting feature that is adaptable to local reference environments and allows operators to create three types of scripts: digital photos, chat texts, and browser links. The digital photos are static images that can be pictures of staff, library service points, floor plans, visuals of campus locations, etc. They appear in the top left corner on the user's browser. Chat text of those phrases or instructions an operator uses repetitively can be created and stored for later use. Double-clicking on a phrase moves it to the user's chat box. Browser links are used as short cuts for URL sharing of commonly used Web sites.

A new rollout target date was set for the beginning of spring semester, January 22, 2002. A Web page of information was created for remote users. The page included an FAQ section and embedded scripts for downloading and installing the IE and Netscape companion on the end user's PC. Later the Netscape companion was dropped from the site because it still was less stable than the IE companion, and because it required too many instructions for the end user to follow. The Library Technology Group was not prepared to support it for off-campus users.

FIGURE 4. Convey Agent Pro Interface

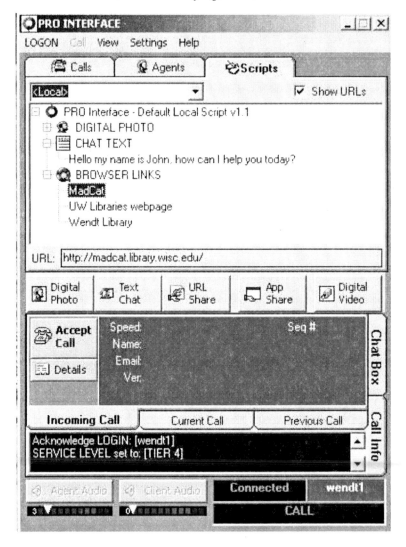

The rollout plan was set to occur in two-week increments. First, the Live Help button was placed on the Web pages of all participating campus libraries (see Figure 5). Later, the call button was added to MadCat, the libraries' OPAC. The persistent button was added to commercial resources, beginning with SilverPlatter/WebSPIRS resources because the content is loaded locally.

FIGURE 5. UW-Madison Libraries Homepage with Live Help Call in Progress

Every two weeks buttons were added to more vendors, until most of the primary resources for every discipline had a persistent button. Over 100 of UW-Madison Libraries primary resources now have Live Help available for end users. All the various resources fall into one of three groups: Web site, MadCat, or Database. Operators see the resource group name along with the caller's e-mail address before they answer a call, thereby getting a tip-off to the type of question based on the origin of the call. Group labels are also used for statistical analysis.

The marketing and advertising of the service was deliberately low key during the pilot project. The campus library service area extends to approximately 600 PCs and the persistent button appears on every page of the library Web site, the OPAC, and many primary commercial databases. The planning group had decided to be cautious about the customer load on librarian/operators and the network and to stay publicly silent about the service. The first legitimate call (see Figure 6) came on the second day, through the OPAC.

STATISTICS FROM SPRING SEMESTER IMPLEMENTATION

During the spring semester over 1,000 calls were logged to the service. Three-fourths of those were for training purposes. Some generalizations can be made about the remaining 250 legitimate user sessions.

Status of the Call (see Figure 7). "Status of the call" indicates whether or not the call was answered or if the connection failed before the librarian could answer the call. The "unanswered calls" occurred during non-service times. Librarians would often log in to the system during those times for testing and training. End user calls that were answered are reflected in the time of day chart.

Where Calls Originated (see Figure 8). Library Web pages generated by far the greatest number of calls, 72%. It could be postulated that many callers desired help in the early stages of their information search. One reason that the databases generated so few calls was the timing of the rollout sequence of the persistent buttons. The Live Help button was added to ProQuest Research Library and Academic Search late in the semester. Now that over 100 databases have the calling button it is anticipated that the number of calls from those resources will increase.

Calls Answered by Library (see Figure 9). The science libraries answered 58% of the calls, with the Wendt (engineering) Library accounting for more than a quarter of the answered calls. It could be speculated that the sciences in

FIGURE 6. Log of First Call to UW-Madison Live Help Service

SeqNumber	IPAddress	LoggedTime	AcceptedTime	HangupTime	GroupName	UserName	email
38701	144.92.164.200	1/23/2002 2:35:47 PM	1/23/2002 2:36:01 PM	1/23/2002 2:52:50 PM	MadCat	memorial2	XXXXXX@XXXXXXX

FIGURE 7. Chart Showing Statistics for Status of Calls

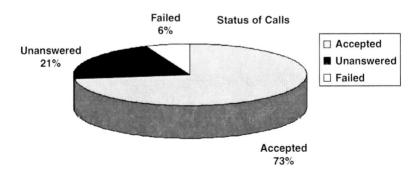

FIGURE 8. Chart Showing Statistics of Where Calls Originated

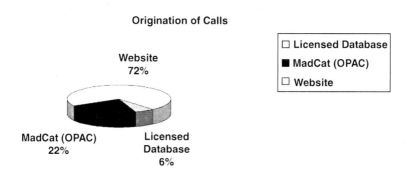

Origination of Calls

Website
72%

MadCat (OPAC)
22%

Licensed
Database
6%

☐ Licensed Database
■ MadCat (OPAC)
☐ Website

FIGURE 9. Chart Showing Statistics for Calls Answered by Library

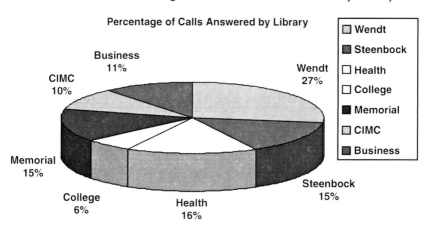

Percentage of Calls Answered by Library

Business
11%

CIMC
10%

Wendt
27%

Memorial
15%

College
6%

Health
16%

Steenbock
15%

☐ Wendt
■ Steenbock
☐ Health
☐ College
■ Memorial
☐ CIMC
■ Business

general, and engineers specifically, adapt more quickly to new technologies. It is expected that the College Library (undergraduate) will see a future increase in calls once late night hours are added and an advertising campaign directed toward the undergraduates is in place.

Answered Calls by Month (see Figure 10). This chart mirrors the trends seen with the reference desk traffic and building gate counts. March and April are usually the busiest service months. The March numbers would possibly have been higher except that the UW's spring break occurred that month.

Calls by Time of Day (see Figure 11). Forty-four percent of calls came between 3:00 p.m. and 6:00 p.m. with a trend upward from 7:00 p.m. through 9:00 p.m. This may indicate a need for more service hours beyond 9:00 p.m.

FIGURE 10. Chart Showing Calls Answered by Month

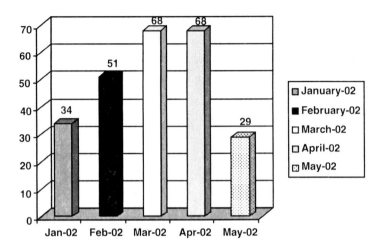

Answered Calls by Month

The thirty or so calls answered before 1:00 p.m. occurred during testing, training, or by appointment. Wendt Library taught a morning credit course using WebCT courseware, and students were given extra credit if they consulted with a librarian remotely through Live Help.

With the software and system in place, library staff members have high expectations for increased use of the service during the next semester. A number of elements are in place to deliver on those expectations. First, the campus library network is switching from the Netscape to the Internet Explorer browser for fall 2002. Testing and reports from other institutions convince library staff that the companion will not have any adverse effect when used with Internet Explorer. Second, the call button has been added to all major discipline resources, and about a thousand computers lab machines will have the companion software. Third, all participating staff have a common understanding of the system and experience with it. Library staff members have created a set of Web-based aides for reference librarians that will allow them to quickly locate databases and electronic resources in disciplines outside of their area of expertise. Lastly, a thorough, multi-level promotional campaign will be deployed.

A Convey Systems representative who was involved in the project has developed a set of marketing campaign planning guidelines for Convey customers. Over the summer of 2002, staff members have demonstrated the service during the orientation sessions for transfer students, international students, and

FIGURE 11. Chart Showing Calls by Time of Day

Number of Calls by Time of Day

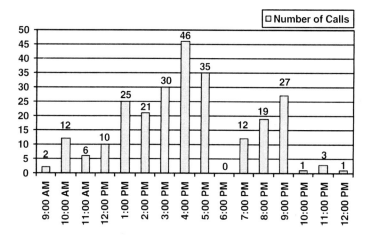

new graduate students. The fall campaign has been designed around the service logo (see Figure 12), reinforcing the message of Live Help through traditional signage, campus newspaper articles, posters, banners, designer mouse pads, and top-level Web page placement.

OTHER LIBRARY APPLICATIONS

The utility of this unique Web communication tool for virtual reference is amply demonstrated. Libraries could also adapt this technology to other traditional and innovative services, wherever a librarian's virtual presence is needed. Wendt Library has successfully employed Convey's technology to support a Web-based credit course developed with WebCT. The bibliographic instruction coordinator for Wendt Library uses the system for consulting sessions with distance education students in the Master of Engineering in Professional Practice program. The Live Help button will be added to the campus portal under the MyLibrary selection to assist end users with resource selection.

Virtual reference help is most useful at the time of need in the classroom or during the hands-on part of bibliographic instruction sessions. Librarians can supply backup assistance to a number of remote computer labs while multi-tasking from their offices. With the voice over IP feature, a librarian can guide a tentative new user through database tutorials or subject Webliographies.

Staff members are currently experimenting with Convey's video applica-

FIGURE 12. Live Help Promotional Graphic

tion feature to add a dynamic visual element for static print collections (see Figure 13). The Wendt Library print reference collection was selected as the basis for an on-demand video service. An end user can access the tables of contents of a print resource from a link in the OPAC and identify a section to view. The persistent button feature insures that every table of contents file will display the persistent call button. The URLs for the tables of contents have been registered with Convey to link calls only to the Wendt Library operator logins. Wendt reference staff will retrieve the resource for the caller and place it under a special Web camera. The video is shared with the end user who identifies the proper page(s) to view. Once the requested page or data is identified the librarian captures the page and forwards the image to the caller. This "instant library loan" can be applied to any number of non-circulating collections or archives if they have a digital component with a unique URL or domain name. Every item in the collection can have a virtual presence at the time of user need.

FIGURE 13. Graphic of "Instant Library Loan" Transaction

Some of the peripherals used for this "instant library loan" project include the HP Capshare handheld scanner, the Canon Vizcam Webcam, the Winnov video conferencing kit, the Visioneer StrobePro scanner and the Labtech headset with microphone.

Convey also offers a feature called the remote e-mail link (see Figure 14). They will advise customers with the setup of a personal Web page that will automatically download the companion software and place a call to a designated login. Staff can add the URL to their signature files and set specific times when they are available to receive calls. Virtual office hours are another useful mechanism for faculty liaison opportunities or consulting with graduate students in the field.

THE FUTURE

Campus librarians are developing a state-of-the-art reference service at the University of Wisconsin-Madison. An initial exploratory question about the

FIGURE 14. Graphic of E-Mail Link for Direct Access Feature

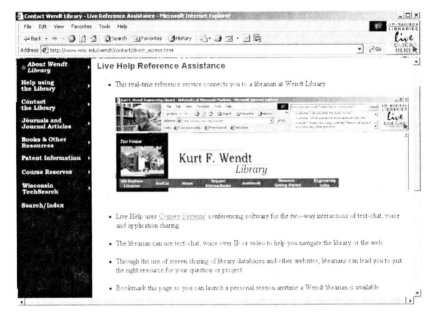

functionality of a new technology product eventually led to the integration of the Convey software product into a worldwide virtual reference service. OCLC has become the library vendor for Convey Systems OnDemand™ software through the QuestionPoint™ service. Convey has given "grandfather" status to its UW-Madison library system relationship. Reference staff will continue to utilize the OnDemand™ software version developed in collaboration with Convey while the range of library applications suitable for this communication tool is explored. Other campus entities such as the admissions office, freshman orientation programs, computer laboratory help desks, and student services have expressed some interest in the Convey products. The campus library is no longer just the center of archived intellectual content. Librarians are truly agents of change, innovators, and facilitators of communication in the virtual world.

LIST OF LIVE HELP PROJECT PARTICIPANTS

Reference Coordinators Committee. Eunice Graupner, Chair, Business Library; Janice Rice and Linda Balsiger, College Library; Peter Cupery, CIMC;

William Ebbot, Law Library; Gerri Wanserski and Christopher Hooper-Lane, Health Science Libraries; David Null, Steven Frye, and Nancy McClements, Memorial Library; Robert Sessions and Gretchen Farewell; Steenbock Library; and John Wanserski, Wendt Library.

Kurt F. Wendt Library Staff. Tom Murray, Director; Amy Kindschi, Head of Faculty and Student Services; Mark McClung, Computer Services; Heather McCullough, Digital/Reference Library Intern; and Sarah Johnston, Digital/Reference Library Intern.

General Library System Staff. Nolan Pope, Associate Director; Steven Daggett and Mitchell Lundquist, Library Technology Group; Edward Van Gemert, Assistant Director for Public Services; and Donald Johnson, Library Communications Office.

UW School of Library and Information Science Student Volunteers. Ronna Hoeper, Tom Durkin, Scott Watkins, Justine Martin, Kristin Partlo, and Heather Daniels.

Convey Systems Inc. John Ingraham, Director of Virtual Reference Projects; Timothy Whitaker, Systems Engineer; Christian Williams, Systems Engineer; and Robert Lee, Software Developer.

WEBLIOGRAPHY

These Web sites have been referred to in the article. They are listed to give the reader additional information on particular aspects of the products or services.

Live Help
(Instant Message/Chat with a librarian in real time from your home or office PC) <http://www.library.wisc.edu/libraries/reference/livehelp/index.html>

Convey Systems, Inc.
<http://conveysystems.com/>

Kurt F. Wendt Library Homepage
<http://www.wisc.edu/wendt/>

Examples of Convey Calling Buttons
<http://www.conveysystems.com/buttons.htm>

John Wanserski's Virtual Office Hours Link (use with IE only)
<http://www.wisc.edu/wendt/livehelp/direct_access.html>

Convey Systems Press Release about QuestionPoint™
<http://www.conveysystems.com/press/CS_Press_5_20.asp>

RefWorks
<http://www.csa2.com/csa/HelpV5/refworks.shtml>

HP Capshare handheld scanner
<http://www.hp.com/cposupport/prodhome/hpcapshare11626.html>

Canon vizcam
<http://www.canonprojectors.com/products/vizcam.html>

Winnov video conferencing kit
<http://www.winnow.com/products/collaboration/index.html>

Visioneer StrobePro scanner
<http://www.visioneer.com/products/sheetfed/nt/>

Labtech headset
<http://www.labtec.com/index.cfm?countryid=1001&languageid=1>

NOTES

1. Abe Anhang and Steve Coffman, "The Great Reference Debate," *American Libraries*, March 2002: 50-4.

2. John V. Richardson Jr., "Reference Is Better Than We Thought," *Library Journal*, April 15, 2000: 41-2.

3. Kelly Broughton, Stefanie Dennis Hunker, and Carol A. Singer. "Why Use Web Contact Center Software for Digital Reference?" *Internet Reference Services Quarterly* 6, no 2 (2001): 1-12.

4. Marc Meola and Sam Stormont, "Real-Time Reference Service for the User: From the Telephone and Electronic Mail to Internet Chat, Instant Messaging, and Collaborative Software," *The Reference Librarian*, no. 67/68 (1999): 30.

5. "The Search Engine Index," Search Engine Watch. Available: <http://searchenginewatch.com/reports/seindex.html>. Accessed: July 9, 2002.

6. Bernie Sloan. "Ready for Reference: Academic Libraries Offer Web-Based Reference; Preliminary Report. Available: <http://www.lis.uiuc.edu/~b-sloan/ready4ref.htm>. Accessed: July 19, 2002.

Managing an Established
Virtual Reference Service

Karen Ciccone
Amy VanScoy

SUMMARY. Virtual reference, no longer a "new thing," has become an integral part of reference services. While implementing a new virtual reference service may not be as difficult now as it was in the past, established services must still grapple with several difficult philosophical, managerial, and policy issues. This article discusses how the North Carolina State University (NCSU) Libraries has dealt with four areas common to developing virtual reference services: getting too many patrons at once, problem patrons, training and quality assessment, and expanding and improving the service. *[Article copies available for a fee from The Haworth Document Delivery Service: 1-800-HAWORTH. E-mail address: <docdelivery@haworthpress.com> Website: <http://www.HaworthPress.com> © 2003 by The Haworth Press, Inc. All rights reserved.]*

KEYWORDS. Virtual reference, problem patrons, training, quality assessment

Karen Ciccone (karen_ciccone@ncsu.edu) is Head, Natural Resources Library, and Amy VanScoy (amy_vanscoy@ncsu.edu) is Assistant Head of Research and Information Services, both at North Carolina State University Libraries.

[Haworth co-indexing entry note]: "Managing an Established Virtual Reference Service." Ciccone, Karen, and Amy VanScoy. Co-published simultaneously in *Internet Reference Services Quarterly* (The Haworth Information Press, an imprint of The Haworth Press, Inc.) Vol. 8, No. 1/2, 2003, pp. 95-105; and: *Virtual Reference Services: Issues and Trends* (ed: Stacey Kimmel, and Jennifer Heise) The Haworth Information Press, an imprint of The Haworth Press, Inc., 2003, pp. 95-105. Single or multiple copies of this article are available for a fee from The Haworth Document Delivery Service [1-800-HAWORTH, 9:00 a.m. - 5:00 p.m. (EST). E-mail address: docdelivery@haworthpress.com].

http://www.haworthpress.com/store/product.asp?sku=J136
© 2003 by The Haworth Press, Inc. All rights reserved.
10.1300/J136v08n01_08

INTRODUCTION

Virtual reference is no longer a new thing. According to Richard Dougherty, "over 1,000 libraries already offer some version of virtual reference."[1] In many libraries, as at the North Carolina State University Libraries, it is now an integral part of reference services. Private companies are also successfully providing software and outsourced reference service, and collaborative efforts, such as the Library of Congress' and OCLC's QuestionPoint, continue to grow and evolve.

At this point in the history of virtual reference, most of the basic nuts-and-bolts questions have been answered. Many service models have been developed and widely communicated, and librarians working on implementing virtual reference services have a wealth of articles and Web sites to peruse. Software evaluations (such as Phil Blank's online feature comparison),[2] practical advice (such as Anne Lipow and Steve Coffman's training manual, *Establishing a Virtual Reference Service*),[3] service models (such as those described by Michael McClennan and Patricia Memmott),[4] and case studies (such as Josh Boyer's "Virtual Reference at NCSU Libraries: The First One Hundred Days")[5] make the process of implementing a virtual reference service fairly straightforward. Bernie Sloan's *Digital Reference Services Bibliography*,[6] with well over 400 entries, attests to the quantity of information available on this topic.

The NCSU Libraries launched its live, online reference service on January 8, 2001. Since then, the Libraries has completed over 3,980 online reference transactions, for an average of 221 sessions per month. Use of the service has grown dramatically since it was introduced, quickly eclipsing in popularity the long-established e-mail reference service (see Figure 1).

During the long, busy months of operating the service, unexpected problem situations arose, pointing out gaps in the Libraries' policies and guidelines. For example, staff had to deal with requests from too many patrons at once, and with the problem of abusive patrons. Along with the everyday management of the service, service managers also began exploring how to expand and improve it. They discussed how to measure quality and how to train staff to be effective at delivering virtual reference, and they brainstormed about where the service should be going. This article will look at how the NCSU Libraries dealt with four areas common to developing virtual reference services: getting too many patrons at once, problem patrons, training and quality assessment, and expanding and improving the service.

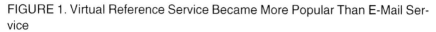

FIGURE 1. Virtual Reference Service Became More Popular Than E-Mail Service

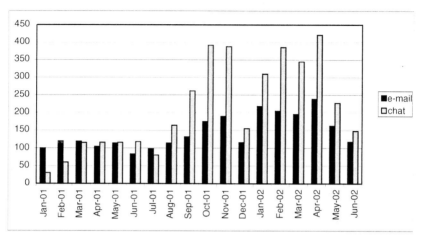

GETTING TOO MANY PATRONS AT ONCE

Early on, the decision was made that virtual reference service would be neither a pilot project nor a special, separate service. There was a commitment to integrate this new mode of providing assistance into the existing suite of reference services. Based on this decision, all reference staff, librarians and paraprofessionals alike, were trained to provide virtual reference. The Off-Site Services room was set up to serve all remote reference patrons, responding to requests by phone, e-mail, and chat. Staff anticipated that virtual reference would grow, and grow it did.

The problem arose not with the number of patrons, but with what one staff member described as the "feast or famine" nature of the service. If the patrons were distributed evenly over all of the hours of service, the traffic could be managed easily. In fact, based on the average number of patrons served per day or per hour, the service doesn't look too busy. In April 2002, a typically busy month, staff members assisted an average of thirteen patrons per day, for an average of only one patron per hour. But just as at the in-person reference desk, certain hours are busier than others. The busiest hours tend to be noon to 5:00 p.m., when there is an average of 1.5 to 1.8 patrons per hour. But during any given hour the number of transactions ranges from zero to nine, with many staff assisting four to five patrons per hour. One other complicating factor is that in contrast to the in-person desk, patrons can't see that the staff member is industriously helping other patrons. The virtual patron just waits in a vacuum and wonders what's taking so long.

One of the solutions that some libraries use to deal with an overwhelming number of users in the face of limited resources is authentication. Authentication software can allow a patron to access a database or other resource based on an IP address or based on a user name and password that identifies the patron as a legitimate library user. As it is used for virtual reference, a patron must be identified as a legitimate user in order to submit a question.

The Libraries' virtual reference statistics suggest that implementing authentication for virtual reference would immediately reduce traffic by 18%. At first, this seemed like a welcome solution. Since virtual reference is extremely time-consuming, compared with in-person reference, the Libraries could legitimately restrict this premium service to primary clientele–NC State students, faculty, and staff. Other forms of reference service would still be provided to all users (see Figure 2).

Although authentication seemed to be an attractive solution to the problem of juggling too many simultaneous patrons, there were serious reservations about restricting the service to only university affiliates. The Libraries is strongly committed to its land-grant mission to serve the citizens of North Carolina. The Libraries is also a Federal Documents Depository Library and a Patent and Trademark Depository Library, with a commitment and mission to serve the general public in using these collections. When staff provide in-person service at the reference desk, they pride themselves on providing at least

FIGURE 2. Non-Affiliated Patrons Make Up a Large Percentage of Virtual Reference Users

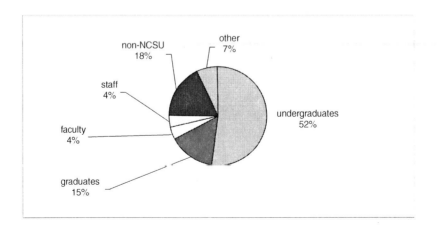

basic assistance and instruction to all users no matter how busy they are. Although virtual reference is a more time-intensive service, patrons tend to see it as merely a virtual version of the in-person reference desk. Therefore, service standards and policies for virtual reference should be as similar as possible to those for in-person reference.

Simple, easy solutions were developed that would have a big impact on the ability of staff to manage busy hours. For example, staff members were encouraged to use scripted messages, such as "Please hold for a minute. I will be right with you." With two clicks of a mouse, a staff member can send a patron the message that her request has been received and that she will be helped as soon as someone is available. This is the virtual equivalent of acknowledging a patron waiting in line at the reference desk. Scripted messages can also offer the patron other options for service, such as sending an e-mail query.

Another solution is to use instant messaging to call quickly for backup assistance. An Instant Messenger (IM) Buddy List was created for all reference staff, and staff were encouraged to use IM to request assistance from other staff at their desks. On the few occasions when staff members have requested backup, the system has worked well. It is easy for staff members sitting at their desks to log in and help out their colleagues. A more common use of IM is consulting with another librarian. Staff members at the reference desk usually have a colleague nearby with whom to collaborate. The Off-Site Services room, on the other hand, is staffed with only one person. Staff members use IM to overcome this isolation and collaborate with colleagues at their desks.

Several informal meetings were held for staff to discuss the issue of managing multiple requests and shared suggestions for handling the traffic. One idea that emerged from these meetings was to measure how busy the Off-Site Services shift really is. It's easy to see how many virtual reference transactions are handled during a given hour, but in order to appropriately staff this service point, service managers need to know whether the single staff member can handle these transactions along with e-mail and phone calls. During one week staff recorded the number of times per hour that virtual reference, phone, and e-mail interfered with each other and how busy the service point felt: OK, hectic, or unmanageable. Some of the hours were hectic, but none were unmanageable. The three types of reference service seem to conflict with each other only occasionally. These findings indicate that the Libraries can continue to use the current strategies for managing traffic without restricting service to reduce the number of transactions.

The Libraries continues to collect and analyze statistics on who is using the service. If the service continues to grow or the number of non-affiliated patrons increases, authentication or other solutions may be reconsidered.

PROBLEM PATRONS

Reference staff members occasionally have to deal with problem situations at the reference desk and occasionally have to delete an inappropriate e-mail message. However, problem patrons are of greater concern with virtual reference because of the time and effort it takes to respond to a question. Some libraries are cautious about starting a virtual reference service for fear that it will be abused. Experience shows that overall, patrons are polite and appreciative. The service was available for ten months before a problem patron situation arose. Although dealing with this one patron was a relatively small problem, service managers realized that better guidelines and policies were needed to help deal with such situations.

Staff initially tolerated the problem patron, finding the behavior annoying but not threatening. However, when the patron repeatedly sent the same request and began using abusive language, a legal authority was consulted. The North Carolina General Statute on cyberstalking (§ 14-196.30) states: "It is unlawful for a person to . . . electronically communicate to another repeatedly, whether or not conversation ensues, for the purpose of abusing, annoying, threatening, terrifying, harassing, or embarrassing any person." So an offense as mild as repeatedly annoying the staff and abusing the purpose of the service is considered illegal.

Although staff normally holds sacred a patron's privacy, an abusive person in cyberspace does not have a right to anonymity. A staff member contacted the patron's Internet Service Provider (ISP) and reported that one of its subscribers was abusing the service. Since this violates the ISP's rules of use, they sent him a warning. After three more abusive requests from this person the next week, the ISP was contacted again. A second warning from the ISP was apparently enough, because the patron ceased sending the messages.

Partly in response to this incident, the libraries created a document outlining rules for use of the NCSU Libraries that include the virtual environment as well as the physical facility. The introduction states that, "The following rules apply in all public areas of the Libraries and in its online service environments." The rules for use of computers clearly state, "Harassment is not permitted while interacting with library staff at any service point, whether in person or through technologies provided for interaction and assistance such as electronic mail or computer conferencing."[7]

These guidelines are now part of the reference training program, so that staff understand what to do if they encounter inappropriate behavior. This includes reporting the incident to their managers and knowing that they should "hang up" as soon as a patron becomes abusive.

TRAINING AND QUALITY ASSESSMENT

After becoming comfortable with providing virtual reference service, service managers began to consider the issue of quality assessment. In general, patrons are thrilled with the service, as evidenced by the typical interjections, "cool" and "awesome." The reports generated by the software show that staff members have responded to 99% of the patrons requesting service, which also indicates that the service is performing well. However, although staff and service managers occasionally review the transcripts of the virtual reference interactions to gauge a general standard of service, no formal quality assessment has been conducted.

One of the challenges is not having a clear definition of quality as it applies to virtual reference. John Richardson, Visiting Scholar at Library Systems and Services, LLC (LSSI), developed a set of quality criteria for the Samuel Swett Green Award for Exemplary Virtual Reference. He based these virtual reference criteria on in-person reference criteria such as asking open-ended questions and having a courteous disposition. But how appropriate are these standards to the virtual environment? Research has not been conducted on what patrons really value in terms of virtual reference. Are the standards for courteousness, for example, different in a chat interaction than they are in person? Use of slang and a terse, abbreviated style might give an in-person patron the impression that a librarian is rude and uninterested in the question. However, in a virtual transaction, the same manner might be much appreciated by the patron and seen as responsive.

In defining quality for the service, service managers began by discussing what the service should really do. Initially, it was assumed that the questions received would be similar to those received over the telephone–primarily ready reference questions or electronic access troubleshooting. Instead patrons use virtual reference as a replacement for in-person reference–some ask short questions, but others request basic instruction or in-depth assistance (see Figure 3).

Since online interactions can take significantly more time than in-person questions, should they be limited to ready reference questions only? Or should virtual reference attempt to provide the same service as in-person reference? Looking at the statistics, it is obvious that patrons consider virtual reference to be simply an online reference desk. Although conducting a thorough reference interview and providing research instruction via a "chat" interface can sometimes be frustrating, staff members tend to agree with the patrons. In addition, one of the main incentives to purchase high-end virtual reference software was to improve reference service to distance learners. In many cases, remote reference is a distance learner's only option for assistance, and virtual reference of-

FIGURE 3. Many Virtual Reference Questions Are Not Short Answer

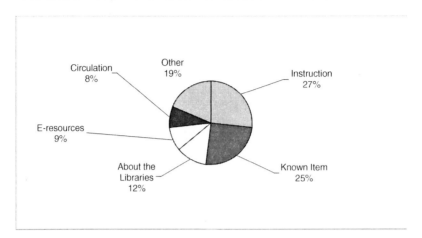

fers features that the telephone and e-mail do not. Therefore, virtual reference should mimic the services of the in-person desk.

The first step toward ensuring quality was to establish a formal training program that covered more than just using the virtual reference software. In the first part of the Libraries' Off-Site Services training, trainers talk about the philosophy of the service and how it fits in with other reference services. Trainees read Anderson, Boyer, and Ciccone's article "Remote Reference Services at the North Carolina State University Libraries," which clearly explains the history and values of the NCSU Libraries' telephone, e-mail, and virtual reference services.[8] Trainers discuss strategies for dealing with many patrons at once or problem patrons. In the second part of the training, trainees practice responding to virtual reference requests. While the trainee monitors a test queue, experienced staff members send typical questions and then provide feedback to the trainee. For many staff members, their first few virtual reference transactions are tense, nerve-wracking experiences. Offering them hands-on practice has been an effective way to help them build confidence as well as skill with the software.

Service managers continue to look for an assessment tool for effectively measuring the quality of service.

EXPANDING AND IMPROVING THE SERVICE

Even an established virtual reference service presents many questions and challenges. After extending hours into evenings and weekends, formalizing the training program, training new staff in branch libraries to assist with the service, and working with the vendor to collect additional data about patrons and categorize transactions by subject, service managers began to consider next steps. New issues are being considered, such as collaborating with colleagues at other libraries, creating a knowledge base of reference answers, and exploring new technologies for virtual reference.

Collaborating with Other Libraries

Along with the growth of interest in virtual reference came the simultaneous growth of interest in collaborative reference services. Librarians have a history of productive collaboration in other areas of the profession, and it is exciting to see interest in cross-library partnerships to better serve users.

Librarians from the NCSU Libraries have met with librarians from the University of North Carolina at Chapel Hill's libraries and the Duke University Libraries to discuss virtual reference issues, including collaboration. Because the NCSU Libraries already collaborates with these institutions in the areas of collection management and document delivery, it seems natural to ask how collaboration in the area of virtual reference might benefit patrons. Factors to consider in deciding whether or not to collaborate in this area are the libraries' values and missions, as well as the various reference services offered by each library system. Whether or not there is value to be gained from collaboration remains to be determined.

One issue to consider in determining the value to be gained from collaborating is to what extent collaborative reference could be effective among academic institutions, given the institutional and curricular context in which questions arise. The questions received by academic libraries, unlike those generally received by public libraries, often refer to specific assignments that staff are prepared to answer. Many of the questions also require knowledge of a specific institution's policies, services, and collections. How would librarians from other institutions be trained to answer these types of questions for NCSU patrons, and how would the quality of the transactions be controlled?

In order to experiment with collaborative virtual reference, the libraries will need to devise procedures and techniques to help staff deal with the challenge of responding to reference questions from patrons of multiple institutions. Cheat sheets will be created with links to local service and policy information, passwords, and other answers to institution-specific information to assist the non-local librarian. Since so many of the questions received involve instruction or in-depth reference, the libraries might also want to share copies of recurring assignments and create a listserv for questions that come up repeatedly at the various reference desks. Librarians from the various institutions may also want to spend time at each other's reference desks to get a feel for the types of questions received and service standards.

Would a Knowledge Base of Reference Answers Be Useful?

A knowledge base could be a useful tool for answering ready reference questions. In considering whether or not to undertake such a project, service managers discussed how useful it might be in relation to how expensive or time-consuming it might be to create. If virtual reference staff are primarily answering questions and making referrals, then a knowledge base would be extremely useful and in the long run the time spent creating it would be worthwhile. However, if staff members are primarily conducting reference interviews and instructing patrons, then a knowledge base would be of limited use.

Since staff tend to do some of both of these activities at the NCSU Libraries, service managers decided that a knowledge base would be useful, but is probably not the best use of time in the immediate future. Simpler solutions such as pre-scripted phrases and pre-programmed Web pages can serve the same function of making common quick reference questions easier to answer. A higher priority is therefore to focus on creating these simpler tools, as well as continuing to improve the Libraries' Web pages so that patrons can more easily help themselves.

Exploring New Technologies

Judging from the popularity of virtual reference service, it is a useful tool for many patrons. It has proven to be a wonderful solution to two reference problems: serving distance learners and troubleshooting remote access problems. But it has also proven to be popular for standard reference desk questions. Obviously, patrons enjoy being able to access the reference desk from wherever they are when the need for assistance arises.

As helpful as virtual reference software has been for simulating the reference desk, it is really a poor replacement for the complex interpersonal communication that occurs so effortlessly in an in-person transaction, or even over the phone. Much of the reference interaction is lost as librarians and patrons struggle to type their thoughts and study each other's words for the nuances that facial expression and tone of voice usually convey.

Voice over IP will help by including tone of voice in the transaction, and eventually video conferencing may allow virtual reference to provide even more of the same degree of interactive, multi-modal communication that patrons enjoy at the reference desk. The Libraries looks forward to experimenting with these new technologies as they become available.

CONCLUSION

Virtual reference no longer has the mark of a "fad" and has become just another facet of the services that reference librarians provide. As libraries' virtual reference services mature, there are still issues and problems that even experienced virtual reference providers must deal with. As virtual reference becomes popular, libraries must develop strategies for managing multiple simultaneous requests and the inevitable problem of problem patrons. They must also continue to improve and expand their training and quality assurance programs. The NCSU Libraries has found several practical solutions for these problems and continues to look for ways to improve and expand virtual reference service. This discussion of NCSU libraries' experiences will hopefully help others find practical solutions to their own problems. More exploration of solutions and sharing of suggestions and data will help to establish best practices for virtual reference.

As libraries struggle with these issues related to "chat" reference, they should keep in mind that this is, in fact, only an interim solution. Chat, while it enables reference service to go where it has not gone before, is not the ideal way to provide real-time, online reference. New technologies, such as Voice over IP, will redefine "virtual reference" and provide new challenges over the next few years.

NOTES

1. Richard Dougherty, "Reference Around the Clock: Is It in Your Future?" *American Libraries* 33, no. 5 (May 2002): 44-6.
2. Phil Blank, *Live On Line Reference*. Available: <http://www.lib.duke.edu/reference/liveonlineref.htm>. Accessed: July 24, 2002.
3. Anne Grodzins Lipow and Steve Coffman, *Establishing a Virtual Reference Service* (Berkeley, CA: Library Solutions Press, 2001).
4. Michael McClennen and Patricia Memmott, "Roles in Digital Reference," *Information Technology & Libraries* 20, no. 3 (September 2001): 143-8.
5. Joshua Boyer, "Virtual Reference at the NCSU Libraries: The First One Hundred Days," *Information Technology & Libraries* 20, no. 3 (September 2001): 122-8.
6. Bernie Sloan, *Digital Reference Services Bibliography*. Available: <http://alexia.lis.uiuc.edu/~b-sloan/digiref.html>. Accessed: July 24, 2002.
7. *Rules of Use of the NCSU Libraries*. Available: <http://www.lib.ncsu.edu/administration/policy/libraryuse.html>. Accessed: July 24, 2002.
8. Eric Anderson, Josh Boyer, and Karen Ciccone, "Remote Reference Services at the North Carolina State University Libraries," Available: <http://www.vrd.org/conferences/VRD2000/proceedings/boyer-anderson-ciccone12-14.shtml>. Accessed: July 24, 2002.

Florida Libraries Go Live:
A Look at Chat Reference Services

Gloria Colvin

SUMMARY. Chat reference is quickly becoming a standard reference service in a variety of Florida libraries. This article examines the development of chat reference services in the state's academic and public libraries and compares software, staffing, and patterns of use among various libraries offering this service. Responding to the needs of the rapidly growing numbers of distance learners who needed assistance in using electronic library resources, several of the state university libraries began using commercial customer service software and developing chat reference programs in 2000. In a relatively short time other libraries have seen the need to assist their online users and have embraced the concept. There is growing interest among libraries in the state in forming collaborative partnerships, enabling more libraries to effectively offer chat service. *[Article copies available for a fee from The Haworth Document Delivery Service: 1-800-HAWORTH. E-mail address: <docdelivery@haworthpress.com> Website: <http://www.HaworthPress.com> © 2003 by The Haworth Press, Inc. All rights reserved.]*

KEYWORDS. Virtual reference, chat reference, reference services, libraries–Florida

Gloria Colvin (gcolvin@mailer.fsu.edu) is Statistics and Assessment Coordinator, Florida State University Libraries, 105 Dogwood Way, Tallahassee, FL 32306-2047.

[Haworth co-indexing entry note]: "Florida Libraries Go Live: A Look at Chat Reference Services." Colvin, Gloria. Co-published simultaneously in *Internet Reference Services Quarterly* (The Haworth Information Press, an imprint of The Haworth Press, Inc.) Vol. 8, No. 1/2, 2003, pp. 107-116; and: *Virtual Reference Services: Issues and Trends* (ed: Stacey Kimmel, and Jennifer Heise) The Haworth Information Press, an imprint of The Haworth Press, Inc., 2003, pp. 107-116. Single or multiple copies of this article are available for a fee from The Haworth Document Delivery Service [1-800-HAWORTH, 9:00 a.m. - 5:00 p.m. (EST). E-mail address: docdelivery@haworthpress.com].

INTRODUCTION

The development of real-time interactive reference services in Florida libraries illustrates the rapid change in library services brought about by technological advances. At the outset of the year 2000, no libraries in Florida offered this service. By mid-2002 a variety of types of libraries in the state were providing chat assistance, and the number of libraries offering this service or planning to offer it was steadily rising. "In another year," predicts Jana Ronan, coordinator of the University of Florida's *RefeXpress* service, "it will probably be unusual for a library not to offer chat reference."[1]

By 2000 e-mail reference service had become commonplace in many Florida libraries, and librarians daily answered queries from local users, as well as from people all over the globe. For those needing immediate assistance, though, e-mail was less than adequate. As libraries increasingly made resources available to users electronically, there came a growing need to provide assistance in the use of those resources and to provide it at the time it was needed. Nowhere was this more apparent than in some of the university libraries, where the need to deliver live interactive reference services through the Web to online users became increasingly clear.

DISTANCE LEARNERS

A major impetus for the development of real-time virtual reference in the state university libraries has been the need to serve their growing numbers of online learners. In 1997-1998, 34,563 students took distance and distributed education courses through Florida's public universities. By 2000-2001 the number of students enrolled in courses in which technology was the primary method of instructional delivery increased to 56,198.[2]

To support this emerging distance education program, the state approved funding for the Florida Distance Learning Library Initiative (FDLLI) in 1997-1998. It was a cooperative venture between the state's universities, community colleges, and public libraries and provided for access to electronic resources, document delivery, cooperative borrowing, library user training, and reference assistance for distance learners throughout the state. As part of FDLLI, the Distance Learning Reference and Referral Center (RRC) was established to provide reference assistance and instruction in the use of information resources to distance learners via the Web and a toll-free telephone line.[3] This experience in working with distance learners contributed to the receptiveness of the RRC and the university libraries to using chat software for virtual reference services.

Virtual reference is well suited to this user population since a significant number of these students are located in areas distant from the university in which they are enrolled. Both distance learners and those online students who are physically on the campus access many library resources electronically via the Web. A natural result is the need to receive assistance from a librarian as they search the Web, use electronic journals and e-books, and navigate the wealth of electronic databases available to them.

The University of Florida pioneered its first virtual reference service in spring 2000, followed soon after by the University of South Florida and the RRC. With the recent disbanding of the RRC due to budget cuts, each university has had to assume the responsibility of providing reference assistance to its distance learners. Of the eleven publicly funded universities in the state, four (University of Florida, University of South Florida, University of Central Florida, and Florida International University) currently provide live virtual reference services and others are in the process of developing such a service.

UNIVERSITY OF FLORIDA

Librarians at the University of Florida (UF) first experimented with MOO-based software, multi-user shareware with a basic chat component, in spring 2000. It was an inexpensive method, requiring additional programming to adapt it for Web use, and it lacked many of the interactive capabilities that characterize current chat software.

As they recognized the limitations of the MOO-based software, librarians at UF searched for software that would provide more functionality and selected NetAgent™, software initially designed for commercial use by call centers. (It is now being marketed to libraries as Divine Virtual Librarian and has been purchased by several library systems in North America.) With NetAgent™ librarians are able to send messages and to push Web pages to a user's browser. They also have the capability of observing a user logged into the service conduct a search, in order to provide assistance as needed. Users can watch a librarian demonstrate database searches or navigate a Web site. Potentially librarians can work with up to six users at a time. The software has the capability of sending transcripts of the reference session via e-mail, collecting statistics, generating reports, and tracking information.

In January 2001 UF introduced its new *RefeXpress* service, fueled by NetAgent™, on a limited basis. During the academic year the *RefeXpress* service is now available from 9:00 a.m. to 9:00 p.m. Monday through Thursday, and from 9:00 a.m. to 5:00 p.m. on Friday. Peak times are between 11:00 a.m. and 2:00 p.m. and from 6:30 p.m. through 9:30 p.m. Thirty-five librarians and paraprofessionals from campus libraries take turns answering questions from their offices or homes.

The service is targeted at persons affiliated with the university and those using UF collections. It has been marketed extensively to students through classes, campus e-mail lists, posters, and flyers. Since its introduction, the volume of questions has steadily increased. In 2001 *RefeXpress* recorded 1,140 questions. Within the first half of 2002 alone, more than 900 questions were submitted.[4]

UNIVERSITY OF SOUTH FLORIDA

When the University of South Florida (USF) initiated its Virtual Library Reference Chat service in September 2000, it used the ConferenceRoom Professional Edition software by WebMaster. This inexpensive software was easy to use, functioned much the same way as instant messaging systems, and required no downloads on the part of the user. Librarians could supply information or refer someone to a source by typing the information. URLs appeared as live links so that the user could browse the Web page, but librarians didn't have the capability of pushing a page to the person's computer or the ability to guide a search. The software could accommodate a large number of simultaneous users, so it had the advantage of allowing librarians to conduct chat sessions for entire classes at the same time.

In March 2002 the USF library began to use more sophisticated software from RightNow Technologies for its virtual reference service. Several other departments on campus were using this commercial customer support software to offer real-time services, and site licensing allowed the library to use it as well. The common chat interface among the various campus departments makes it easier for USF students to use the library's reference service.

The expanded capabilities of the software offer co-browsing and the ability to push pages to a user's computer. Potentially there can be multiple simultaneous users, limited only by the availability of librarians to staff the service. The software provides statistical reports and can manage e-mail. Session transcripts are added to a knowledge base.

The hours for the Live Assistance service have expanded from 9:00 a.m. to 12:00 p.m. on weekdays to include afternoon hours from 2:00 to 4:00 Monday through Friday and evening hours from 7:00 through 11:00 on Wednesday and Sunday. Questions are accepted from anyone regardless of affiliation. When the service was first offered the number of questions for an entire semester totaled about 30. In spite of little promotion of the service, the number of sessions in March, April, and May 2002 averaged 110 per month or about four questions per day.[5]

UNIVERSITY OF CENTRAL FLORIDA

The University of Central Florida (UCF) library launched its INFOch@t service in January 2002. Using LiveHelper software, librarians are able to chat in real-time, to use scripted responses, and to push pages to client computers. LiveHelper, a commercial customer service tool, is attractively priced, but it lacks some features that librarians would like to have, such as a knowledge base for Frequently Asked Questions and the ability to take over a user's computer to guide a search. Librarians at UCF prefer to rely on their own statistics, rather than those provided by LiveHelper, because the software combines visits by browsers with actual chat sessions.

In its first six months the service logged about 25 sessions per week. Almost all users are affiliated with UCF. Statistics indicate that about 50% of users connect from computers on campus, including a number in the library.

Initially hours for INFOch@t were from 10:00 a.m. through 4:00 p.m. Monday through Friday, but they may be extended until 6:00 p.m. beginning in fall 2002. Seven librarians and one senior library technical assistant take turns staffing the service. Only one librarian can be logged in at a given time, but he or she can handle more than one chat session at a time. Librarians at UCF, like those at the other university libraries, staff the chat service from their offices and not while they are on the reference desk.[6]

FLORIDA INTERNATIONAL UNIVERSITY

Florida International University (FIU) uses 24/7 Reference software for the virtual reference service it provides through its Everglades Digital Library. Developed especially for library reference transactions, 24/7 Reference incorporates features from commercial customer support software as well as capabilities specifically designed for library use. Librarians can co-browse Web sites with clients and chat in real-time. They are able to send files and pre-scripted messages to users and to transfer users to other librarians who are logged into the system. No user downloads are required. The software is available in Spanish, a real advantage in serving the largely Hispanic population in the area where the university is located.

Another advantage of 24/7 Reference is its extensive statistical capabilities. It provides full-text transcripts of chat sessions, tracks URLs to indicate where a person found a link to the service, and constructs historical profiles of past questions if the person is a return user. At FIU the full-text transcripts are e-mailed to the user and are also reviewed and shared with other librarians as illustrations of good and bad sessions and unique chat lingo. They also provide evidence of frequently asked questions and alert librarians to information resources that could be added to the library's Everglades Digital Library.

FIU has focused on marketing this service in the virtual environment since that is where most of its users are. Placement of numerous prominent links on Web pages and references in Everglades-related electronic discussion groups have generated increased activity. In designing the Web site the idea of linking to the virtual reference service through a single, central portal was rejected in favor of placing multiple links throughout the Web site. This decision was based on the belief that people want to ask questions where they are on the Web rather than having to search for the place to ask questions. According to chat reference coordinator Megan Waters, the number of questions increased twofold when "clear, concise, catchy links to the service" were placed everywhere. E-mail traffic has also increased since a link to the library's e-mail reference service is provided when a librarian in not available online.

FIU's virtual reference service attracts a multitude of different users, including K-12 students across the country, scientists working with the national Park Service, FIU students and faculty, government workers with the Army Corps of Engineers and other agencies, artists, authors, filmmakers, and tourists. Information on users is gathered from e-mail address suffixes (i.e., .gov, .org, .com), and voluntary login information, as well as from content exchanged during reference interviews.[7]

COMMUNITY COLLEGE LIBRARIES

Interest in real-time virtual reference extends to the state's community colleges, which also offer a wealth of electronic resources to their constituencies. At least two, Gulf Coast Community College and St. Petersburg College, currently offer real-time virtual reference service. The College Center for Library Automation (CCLA), which provides support for the community colleges' automated services and resources, is working on an initiative to develop a collaborative live reference network that would involve all 28 of the state's community colleges.

Gulf Coast Community College

Gulf Coast Community College has offered real-time virtual reference since early 2001. Originally the library used Real Live Helper software, but it has since replaced it with RealTimeAide. This inexpensive software is available for a modest one-time charge and comes with a lifetime license. It operates much like a chat room, but has the capabilities of pushing pages to a user's computer and taking control of a remote machine. Librarians at Gulf Coast don't use the latter feature due to concerns about privacy.

The service was initiated to support the school's 4,000 distance learners, but based on IP addresses, librarians have discovered that many of the system's users come from within the library building. The service has not been widely promoted and is not used heavily, averaging only two questions a day. Librarians observe that students prefer to call a toll-free number or to e-mail questions at this point.

Currently the service is available from 9:00 a.m. through 9:00 p.m. Monday through Thursday, from 9:00 a.m. through 3:00 p.m. on Friday, and from 1:30 p.m. through 4:30 p.m. on weekends. Four librarians take turns staffing it when they are on the reference desk. If the librarian on duty is unable to assist with a query when the person logs on, the session is transferred to a designated alternate.[8]

St. Petersburg College

St. Petersburg College introduced its real-time virtual reference service in summer 2002. Using LivePerson Pro customer support software, librarians are able to push Web pages and URLs, to chat in real-time, and to use scripted responses. The software does not allow co-browsing and does not provide for sending transcripts of sessions. The service is staffed from 1:00 p.m. through 3:00 p.m. Monday through Friday and on Sunday from 1:00 p.m. through 5:00 p.m.[9]

PUBLIC LIBRARIES

Public libraries are beginning to see the possibilities that virtual reference holds for their users. The Broward County Public Library, one of the largest public library systems in the state, has leased two seats with 24/7 Reference and plans to begin offering the service in August 2002. In addition to the software's chat features, an attractive benefit of this software is the ability to provide online instruction and to conduct meetings for up to twenty people simultaneously. The library plans to join the 24/7 Reference consortium of libraries. Libraries in the consortium agree to monitor other sites during specified hours in order to provide extended coverage for the chat service.[10]

Largo Public Library

Largo Public Library, with a staff of three reference librarians, was one of the first public libraries in Florida to offer this service. Librarians wanted to offer a more interactive approach to providing reference service than e-mail afforded in order to assist users as they searched databases, the catalog, or Web sites. The library began using free Human Click software (now owned by Live Person) early in 2001. As an existing customer, the library is still able to use the software free of charge. The software doesn't have any of the advanced features, such as pushing pages, canned responses, or transcripts of sessions.

Hours are limited to 6:00 p.m. through 8:00 p.m. Monday, Wednesday, and Thursday due to limited staff and heavy in-house traffic. Use has been light with only four to five questions handled per month. Questions that are submitted when the service is not staffed are routed to the library's e-mail reference system. Largo librarians would like to join with other libraries in a collaborative effort in order to expand the service and to take advantage of more sophisticated software.[11]

CONSIDERATIONS FOR FUTURE DIRECTIONS

As part of its plan for a statewide virtual library, the Florida Division of Library and Information Services (the State Library) has made implementation of virtual reference statewide a priority. The plan, approved in July 2002, cites the benefits of such a system.

> Virtual Reference is not intended to replace local library reference services, but to expand service by reaching more users, providing more efficient and directed use of human and information resources, and allowing more diversification and less overlap of existing references resources.
>
> A Statewide Virtual Reference implementation could allow users to receive reference assistance outside of normal operating hours; it could also direct users to specialized resources and to librarians with specialized knowledge and information.[12]

Collaborative Efforts

The Tampa Bay Library Consortium (TBLC), one of six multitype library cooperatives in the state, has teamed with the College Center for Library Automation (CCLA) to develop a proposal for a statewide live reference network. If funded, this plan would be integrated as a component of the state's virtual library plan. It would involve all of the state's 28 community college libraries, a number of public and academic libraries belonging to TBLC, and the Florida Division of Library and Information Services Bureau of Library and Network Services. Each participating library would commit to staffing the service for a certain number of the hours per week that the service would be in operation. This would be the first collaborative live reference project in Florida. A second phase of the project would seek to expand the service throughout the state.[13]

Collaborative approaches may be the most effective approach in terms of both cost and staffing for libraries wanting to offer virtual reference services. Cost of software, especially for the systems that offer the more sophisticated features desirable for use in chat reference, is a factor for most libraries. Staffing is also a major concern, especially in a time of budget cuts, staffing shortages, and hiring freezes.

Initiatives such as the TBLC/CCLA Collaborative Reference project, 24/7 Reference, and Question Point offer opportunities for such collaboration and are attracting libraries in Florida and elsewhere. There is also interest among the state's university libraries in plans of the Association of Southeastern Research Libraries (ASERL) to form a consortium for chat reference.[14]

CONCLUSION

Within a relatively short time, virtual reference services are becoming standard library services in the university libraries and are on the verge of being incorporated in many of the state's community college and public libraries. With advances in software design and technological capabilities, growing opportunities for participating in consortia, and the experiences of the libraries that first offered chat serving as a guide, Florida libraries are in the midst of a rapid change in the delivery of reference services.

NOTES

1. Jana Ronan, telephone conversation with author, July 1, 2002.
2. Florida Board of Education, Division of Colleges and Universities, Office of Academic and Student Affairs. April 2002. "An Overview of Distance and Technology Mediated Instruction in the State Universities of Florida." Duplicated.
3. Florida Distance Learning Library Initiative. "Welcome to the Florida Distance Learning Library Initiative." Available: <http://dlis.dos.state.fl.us/dlli>. Accessed: July 26, 2002.
4. University of Florida Libraries. "*RefeXpress.*" Available:<http://refexpress.uflib.ufl. edu>. Accessed: July 16, 2002; Jana Ronan, telephone conversation with author, July 1,

2002; Divine. Available: <http://www.divine.com/servlet/ContentServer?pagename=home>. Accessed: July 15, 2002.

5. University of South Florida, "Welcome to the University of South Florida Virtual Library." Available: <http://helpdesk.acomp.usf.edu>. Accessed: July 13, 2002; Lisa Nickel, "University of South Florida Virtual Reference Services: A Case Study," Available: <http://www.lib.usf.edu/~nickel/chat.htm>. Accessed: June 27 2002; Ilene Frank, e-mail to author, June 27, 2002; Gloria Colvin, "Remote, Accessible, and on Call: Reference Librarians Go Live," *Florida Libraries* 44, no.1 (Spring 2001): 11; Webmaster.com. "ConferenceRoom Products: Professional Edition." Available: <http://www.webmaster.com/products/professional.htm>. Accessed: July 16, 2002; RightNow Technologies. "Live Collaboration." Available: <http://www.rightnow.com/products/live.html>. Accessed: July 16, 2002.

6. University of Central Florida Libraries, "Ask A Librarian." Available: <http://library.ucf.edu/Ask>. Accessed: October 5, 2002; LiveHelper. Available: <http://www.livehelper.com>. Accessed: July 15, 2002; Meredith Semones, e-mail to author, July 2002.

7. Florida International University, "Everglades Digital Library." Available: <http://everglades.fiu.edu>. Accessed: July 2002; Megan Waters, e-mail to author, July 9, 2002; 24/7 Reference. Available: <http://www.247ref.org>. Accessed: July 15, 2002.

8. Gulf Coast Community College, "Librarian on Duty." Available: <http://library.gc.cc.fl.us/contact.htm>. Accessed July 16, 2002; Sue Hatfield, telephone conversation with author, June 26, 2002; Real Time Aide. Available: <http://www.realtimeaide.com/home.htm>. Accessed: July 22, 2002.

9. St. Petersburg College, "Library Online." Available: <http://www.spjc.edu/central/libonline/>. Accessed: July 17, 2002; Patricia Barbier, e-mail to author, July 23, 2002.

10. Louise Lee, e-mail to author, July 15, 2002.

11. Largo Public Library, "Largo Library Virtual Reference Desk." Available: <http://www.tblc.org/largo/virtuallibrary.htm>. Accessed July 24, 2002; Olga Koz, e-mail to author, May 6, 2002; LivePerson. Available: <http://www.liveperson.com>. Accessed July 16, 2002.

12. Florida Division of Information Services, Bureau of Library Development, "Florida Virtual Library Plan Final Draft." Available: <http://dlis.dos.state.fl.us/bld/FL_Virt_Lib_Plan_Final_Draft.pdf>. Accessed: June 16, 2002.

13. Diane Solomon, e-mail to author, May 30, 2002.

14. Association of Southeastern Research Libraries, "ASERL Virtual Reference Project." Available: <http://www.aserl.org/projects/vref/default.htm>. Accessed: July 24, 2002.

Live Reference
in an Academic Health Sciences Library:
The Q and A NJ Experience
at the University of Medicine and Dentistry
of New Jersey Health Sciences Library
at Stratford

Cynthia S. McClellan

SUMMARY. This paper will examine the motivations, considerations, and experiences of librarians at the University of Medicine and Dentistry of New Jersey's (UMDNJ) Health Sciences Library at Stratford (HSL@S), an academic library participating in Q and A NJ, the first 24/7, statewide interactive reference service. This library is in a unique position as the sole health sciences library participating in a statewide project of this scope and breadth. The author gives a unique perspective and demonstrates how multi-type libraries can work together to provide a multitude of benefits to all participants. *[Article copies available for a fee from The Haworth Document Delivery Service: 1-800-HAWORTH. E-mail address: <docdelivery@haworthpress.com> Website: <http://www.HaworthPress.com> © 2003 by The Haworth Press, Inc. All rights reserved.]*

KEYWORDS. Q and A NJ, virtual reference collaboration, health sciences libraries

Cynthia S. McClellan (mcclelcs@umdnj.edu) is Public Services Librarian, UMDNJ Health Sciences Library, Stratford.

[Haworth co-indexing entry note]: "Live Reference in an Academic Health Sciences Library: The Q and A NJ Experience at the University of Medicine and Dentistry of New Jersey Health Sciences Library at Stratford." McClellan, Cynthia S. Co-published simultaneously in *Internet Reference Services Quarterly* (The Haworth Information Press, an imprint of The Haworth Press, Inc.) Vol. 8, No. 1/2, 2003, pp. 117-126; and: *Virtual Reference Services: Issues and Trends* (ed: Stacey Kimmel, and Jennifer Heise) The Haworth Information Press, an imprint of The Haworth Press, Inc., 2003, pp. 117-126. Single or multiple copies of this article are available for a fee from The Haworth Document Delivery Service [1-800-HAWORTH, 9:00 a.m. - 5:00 p.m. (EST). E-mail address: docdelivery@haworthpress.com].

10.1300/J136v08n01_10

INTRODUCTION

The Health Sciences Library at Stratford is one of four campus libraries of the University Libraries system at the University of Medicine and Dentistry of New Jersey system. Staff is composed of five professionals and six paraprofessionals, covering eighty-five hours per week. Located in the southern part of the state, the library serves a core user base comprising faculty, staff, and students of the School of Osteopathic Medicine, the School of Health Related Professions, the School of Nursing, the Graduate School of Biomedical Sciences, the School of Public Health, and the New Jersey Dental School, as well as the administrators and staff of the Kennedy Health System. The campus is growing rapidly, with new programs and departments expanding on UMDNJ's Stratford Campus. Recent newcomers include the UMDNJ School of Public Health, which enrolled its first students in October of 2001. Programs in Advanced Practice Nursing and Psychiatric and Vocational Rehabilitation have been also been added to the campus roster. A five-year campus-wide construction plan is in progress, and is slated to add 97,000 square feet of building space by 2004, supporting the continued growth of educational and clinical programs.

The library also serves a diverse body of remote users. Distance learners, students on clinical rotations, and healthcare providers in various office locations make up this segment. In addition, the library receives a steady flow of in-depth health and medical questions from a variety of local librarians and their users, per consortial contract.

Serving a large, diverse, and dispersed user base engenders communication and training challenges. Creating effective and innovative educational opportunities has long been a chief objective throughout the Library's history. Live, interactive chat technology provides another tool for reaching out to users and assisting them in identifying and using resources effectively–a strong incentive for exploring the benefits of joining the Q and A NJ project. Participation has paved the way to providing enhancements in communication and instructional services, while yielding unanticipated benefits as well.

HISTORY AND BACKGROUND

As noted above, the user base at the UMDNJ HSL@S is a growing, diverse, and evolving body of healthcare students, practitioners, researchers, and support staff. They are specialized information consumers, delving, for the most part, into biomedical resources to serve their clinical and research needs. Supporting this work, the university libraries subscribe to standard biomedical databases such as Medline, CINAHL, and PsycINFO through Ovid™. Standalone databases include ISI Web of Science™ and eMedicine™. Other popular databases include LexisNexis Academic Universe, Alt-HealthWatch, and Health Reference Center (Academic), obtained through VALE (Virtual Academic Library Environment), a statewide consortium of academic libraries.

Another factor influencing the decision to sign on to this project is the HSL@S's history of active participation in multi-type statewide and local library organizations. The library has forged relationships with the South Jersey Regional Library Cooperative (SJRLC), a multi-type library cooperative serving 560 member libraries throughout southern New Jersey over many years. A number of these member libraries routinely call HSL@S for back-up reference assistance in fielding the myriad of detailed (and sometimes indecipherable!) medical questions they receive. HSL@S librarians provide up-to-date, authoritative information from whatever source, print or online, that best addresses the query. The HSL@S also participates, as noted above, in the VALE consortium, the Health Sciences Libraries Association of New Jersey (HSLANJ), and other local groups.

Librarians have long known the value inherent in networking and communication. By establishing effective interlibrary loan networks and delivery systems and reducing costs for database access, consortia have led the way in providing "more bang for the buck" to members. In underwriting and managing this technologically innovative venture, the SJRLC has also extended great value to its membership. The risks and expense that most libraries would find prohibitive if considering service "solo" have been mitigated by the multi-faceted safety net afforded by the Consortium. The structural and emotional support provided by the SJRLC in this project cannot be underestimated; it has provided the impetus for many libraries to move in this direction.

Consortial involvement necessitates committee work, and the author served on the SJRLC's Research and Development Team. This ad hoc committee first convened in August 2000 to address the membership's charge to research and develop new SJRLC services with high marketing potential to the general public, and to position the SJRLC as an R&D incubator. E-books and live, interactive reference services were the most viable candidates for consideration. Live reference quickly percolated to the top of the priorities list. The Team invited Steve Coffman of Library Systems and Services, LLC (LSSI) to visit, and his subsequent demonstration generated a great deal of enthusiasm. Soon afterwards, SJRLC negotiated a contract with LSSI and began tackling the nitty gritty work of getting this complex project off the ground.

MOTIVATIONS AND CONSIDERATIONS

From the outset, the teaching and outreach potential of live reference technology provided the most powerful motivation to become involved. Odd as it may seem, the impetus to institute live reference service did not come from users. As a specialized population accessing specialized, licensed databases, UMDNJ users seemed unlikely to need a reference service geared to the general population. At the HSL@S, traditional reference service is generally conducted by telephone or face-to-face. Other contact points, including an e-mail reference link on the Libraries Web page and the Ask-A-Librarian feature (accessible from within Ovid), are only occasionally utilized. These established communication channels seemed adequate to support users' information needs.

HSL@S librarians questioned whether participation in the SJRLC project was the best way to offer live reference service and speculated on the possibility of establishing a similar or related service, to be administered by the University Libraries. The University Libraries Information Access Committee invited Steve Coffman to demonstrate the software to interested librarians. He accepted the invitation and returned to UMDNJ in March of 2001.

While enthusiasm for the technology was high, the feasibility and expense of providing this service was prohibitive at the time, especially in light of the perceived cost/benefit value to users university-wide. Interest in chat reference continued to grow throughout the New Jersey library community, and Rutgers University hosted a subsequent LSSI demonstration attended by a large group of VALE librarians. The audience reacted enthusiastically but also had many questions and concerns. Shortly thereafter, a VALE Live Reference Committee was established to look into these issues from that consortium's particular perspective. It was clear that a thorough evaluation was required before any consensus or plan would come to fruition.

In the meantime, the SJRLC had worked out many of the details, formulated a contract with LSSI, and outlined the parameters and requirements for participation. The stage was set, and in the fall of 2000–while HSL@S librarians continued to mull the question of participation–the SJRLC moved forward, recruiting the first libraries that would launch the project. UMDNJ librarians debated the pros and cons of participation and considered alternatives, such as participation within the project as a health/medical resource and staffing a separate medical queue for selected hours. Such a queue would require additional funding and administrative costs, and it seemed unwise to institute it at the initial rollout. Q and A NJ shift coverage–an eight-hour per week commitment–was a concern, as librarians at HSL@S were already spread thin. Regular duties would need continued coverage, and progress on other planned projects could not come to a standstill. The excellent quality of service to UMDNJ users could not be compromised during exploration of this new technological area.

Librarians' reference skill levels were also a concern, as the HSL@S's primary focus is healthcare and biomedical information. The potential for variety and depth of questions the Q and A NJ service population would generate was daunting! Would biomedical expertise prove adequate? Also, since the HSL@S did not subscribe to databases standard in public libraries, would the World Wide Web, subscription databases, and print collection be sufficient? Staff felt optimism and a sense of adventure, buoyed by hopes that experience and technical skills would empower them in this new technological environment.

The flip side of this service equation was also troubling and raised many additional questions. Would public librarians properly serve health sciences clinicians, researchers, and students? Would HSL@S users understand that they were contacting a statewide, ready-reference service–not the HSL@S? Would they be disappointed or confused when they did not contact the HSL@S, as the Q and A NJ icon is shared by all participating libraries? Librarians hoped that HSL@S users would understand the scope of the service and not make unreasonable demands on public library colleagues. Would HSL@S users even use the service at all? The prospect of devoting time and energy to a project that local users would rarely use was troubling. Was an immediate need or demand for this service a necessary requirement in deciding to join, or were the "gut feelings" enough justification for jumping in?

Mulling these and related questions, it became clear that this offer was just too good to ignore. Potential risks were minimized by the SJRLC's vision and oversight; they would manage the multitude of administrative details that few libraries would dare approach alone, including technical troubleshooting with LSSI. This provided a huge incentive to libraries that could not otherwise consider such a prohibitively expensive venture. The pluses were many. The HSL@S could debut a "sexy" new service, marketable to users as an enhancement to current resources–perhaps a place where, day or night, a doctor could find homework help for her children, or a student might locate apartment-hunting resources–all with the click from the library's home page. Another great advantage was the potential for adapting the software to meet the HSL@S educational objectives using the Meeting Room function. This function might allow users to gather at remote locations and interact with a librarian instructor for a database training session, for example. At the very least, librarians would gain a fantastic opportunity for hands-on, in-depth exploration of cutting-edge technology. They would also be able to provide an instant enhancement to existing library resources, concurrently contributing to the library community and the public at large. With cost/benefit scales tipping decidedly toward participation, UMD's Stratford librarians decided to seize this chance to get in on the ground floor and thus completed participant agreement form in May 2001. Initial requirements included a commitment of eight hours per week, per library on the live reference cyberdesk and designation of a project manager and technical contact.

EXPERIENCES

Training efforts proceeded quickly, conducted in the centrally located Technical Training Center at the Camden County Library. All librarians received initial basic training, followed by additional scheduled practice sessions to achieve greater levels of comfort and competence. The HSL@S dedicated two librarians to the project. They practiced with each other and also joined additional interlibrary and project-wide practice sessions that the SJRLC facilitated. The HSL@S librarians actively promoted Q and A NJ among the staff, recruiting everyone available to participate as users during this test phase. By the time the Project "went live" in October of 2001, librarians were ready!

Fortunately, numerous libraries signed on, which reduced the original eight-hour per week per library Q and A NJ desk time commitment to a more copasetic six hours, including one two-hour evening shift. At the HSL@S, each librarian covers a full two-hour shift weekly, with the remaining two-hour shift divided. This arrangement has turned out to be quite manageable. While interactive reference duties *cannot* be accomplished effectively while concurrently serving on a traditional reference desk, other tasks–document editing, e-mail, research projects, etc.–lend themselves readily to Q and A NJ shifts. Handy features, such as audible alerts and pop-up window alerts, cue staff when someone is waiting.

Of course, schedules must be juggled, balancing traditional and live reference duties and adjusting for busy and changeable off-desk schedules. The HSL@S circulation supervisor must consider librarians' scheduled Q and A NJ shifts when devising reference desk schedules, incorporating breaks and lunch hours and avoiding scheduling librarians for concurrent live and traditional reference shifts. Additionally, library staff and users need to be alerted of times when librarians are staffing Q and A NJ so that unnecessary interruptions can be avoided. This is not always an easy task, as it may not be evident that work is in progress during these shifts. Signs on office doors serve as notification. Of course, there is always the occasional interruption, but librarians do their best to return quickly, relying on other Q and A NJ colleagues–four librarians generally cover each shift at present–to handle the queues for these brief periods. Coverage for absences due to meetings or vacations can be more challenging, especially when both Q and A NJ librarians must be out of the library. In these cases, the project managers' listserv provides an effective tool of communication, and a posting usually yields a substitute. Larger libraries have been very forthcoming in providing backup assistance, and even smaller libraries with limited staff have assisted on many occasions.

Unforeseen benefits have emerged as a consequence of participation. Reference skills have been enhanced, and participating librarians have become more dexterous at navigating the Web and maneuvering in the Windows operating system (OS) environment. Staff nervousness over locating resources from among the vast array available has dissipated, and self-confidence has grown. The luxury of getting in three hours per week of good, relevant self-directed learning and database practice has proven to be stimulating. Free Internet resources are sufficient to answer most of the questions received, and HSL@S proprietary databases are utilized as needed. Fortunately, vendors have granted permission to the HSL@S (and other Q and A NJ academic libraries) to access to Gale and EBSCO online products, allowing all librarians to better serve Q and A NJ users.

Q and A NJ queries come from all segments of the New Jersey population, all age groups, and all educational levels. The service receives queries from elementary school students and college professors, secretaries and political leaders. Questions touch on all areas of experience and concern: legal, medical, financial, genealogical, entertainment, news–all provide fodder for Q and A NJ librarians. While most questions are the quick, ready-reference variety, others may be thought-provoking, scholarly, and challenging. On rare occasions, Q and A NJ has been inundated by an entire middle school classroom's assignment-related questions, but thankfully such instances are rare. While a small percentage of users exhibit rude or inappropriate behavior, this is not the norm. Many would-be crank callers are put off by a serious reaction to their question, and librarians always have the End Call option at their disposal in the online environment. It is satisfying to find the answer has eluded a user, and to get the occasional, astounded, "Wow! This is great!" response during a session. Such compliments are energizing and reinforce the value inherent in this endeavor to participating librarians.

The Q and A NJ Project Manual <http://www.QandANJ.org/manual/>, created by SJRLC staff, provides an excellent one-stop resource for locating all kinds of project-related information and contacts. As an additional means of communication, SJRLC has established two useful listservs, enabling Q and A NJ librarians to network with colleagues. One is for all participating librarians, and the other is for project managers. Alerts concerning class assignments or repeat questions, scheduling or substitution issues, or handy URLs are communicated in this way. Useful Web sites appearing in these forums are gathered by the New Jersey Statewide Reference Center for inclusion on its Virtual Reference Desk <http://www.camden.lib.nj.us/dbtw-wpd/reference.htm>.

Librarians are also able to utilize the expertise and resources available through other Q and A NJ libraries, referring users to particular libraries or passing a session transcript along to a library that will better meet the information need. At the librarian's discretion, follow up may be completed after the chat session has ended, especially in cases requiring only minimal extra time. Difficult and/or time-consuming questions are referred to the Statewide Reference Center, which serves as a gatekeeper. This center will either continue working on the question or route it to an appropriate library; the HSL@S receives a significant number of health-related questions as referrals. This referral mechanism ensures that librarians are not bogged down with lengthy post-shift research; when a shift is over, it is *over*. SJRLC's helpful "Decision Tree for Complex Questions or Time-consuming Research," available at <http://www.QandANJ.org/manual/decisiontree.htm>, is another useful tool in determining how to proceed with this type of query.

Librarians at the UMDNJ HSL@S have gained technical expertise, expanding on existing database and Windows skills as necessitated by this new environment. Some of the skills learned in the live reference service include conducting a chat interaction, pushing a relevant Web page to users, managing connection problems, finding workarounds to "frame buster" sites (where the use of frames within the HTML code will cause a session to terminate), and sending files of any type. Librarians may join sessions in progress or hand off a question to another librarian as appropriate. With a little maneuvering, multiple queries can be handled by a single librarian. Handy scripted messages, composed by SJRLC or individual librarians, also help streamline reference transactions. Added features promised for the new software release point towards increased interaction with users. Enhanced co-browsing features such as two-way interaction, remote desktop control, and smooth access to proprietary databases are expected to expand teaching opportunities. The HSL@S librarians have just begun to make initial forays in this area, utilizing Q and A NJ for meetings and database training sessions.

USE OF Q AND A NJ

The HSL@S displays the Q and A NJ logo and link prominently on the library's home page <http://www3.umdnj.edu/stlibweb/>, and a special message from the library director announced the date when Q and A NJ went live.

Do HSL@S library users access this resource? While the UMDNJ community was obviously not the prime target population for Q and A NJ, librarians were somewhat disappointed with statistics, which indicated an unequivocal "No" was the answer to this question. Reports generated by university IP addresses indicated only a smattering of queries originating from throughout UMDNJ, mostly from the HSL@S campus. Of course, there is no way to determine if users are utilizing the service from outside of the UMDNJ IP range. Most queries originating from University IPs could be attributed to library staff. A subsequent "quick and dirty" survey conducted in December 2001 on general, non-medical World Wide Web searching indicated that HSL@S users did not realize that the service even existed! This dose of reality provided the library with good information, and staff responded by promoting the service more vigorously. Current promotional efforts include Q and A NJ posters hung in various library locations, bookmarks distributed in several areas, and increased emphasis in library orientations conducted throughout the campus. Though not a primary research tool, Q and A NJ can certainly fill a valuable information niche in the total library services. While librarians do not anticipate that this tool will be heavily used, it is encouraging that library personnel are repeat users. This is a testament to the quality and usefulness of the service, and hopefully use will spread throughout the UMDNJ community.

QUALITY CONTROL

Undoubtedly there is variability in the quality of answers provided by Q and A NJ librarians, but this is also true in traditional reference work. Librarians have wrangled with the reference standards issue for ages, and the question continues today. There is no way of absolutely guaranteeing that users receive quality reference service when they stop by their local public library, and the uncertainty is the same in the Q and A NJ environment. To help ensure quality, Q and A NJ has several mechanisms in place. First, the SJRLC has composed a Competencies Checklist <http://www.QandANJ.org/manual/competencies.htm> as part of the Project Manual, suggesting standards applicable to the virtual reference desk. Secondly, users who access the service are presented with a short survey upon completion of each reference session. Remarks gathered here have been overwhelmingly positive. Library staff members who utilize the service also provide excellent feedback on quality. Perhaps most importantly, all transcripts are distributed weekly to the Q and A NJ project manager whose duty it is to read through them to make sure that they reflect professionalism and quality librarianship. Managers may give feedback to their staff to improve performance, to praise, or to offer additional perspectives on a session. The SJRLC staff has also sampled batches of transcripts to make sure that they adhere to acceptable standards. Procedural, administrative, and service-related issues that continually arise are addressed in monthly meetings with project managers and SJRLC administrators.

CONCLUSION

The bottom line is "Was it worth it?" From the HSL@S's perspective, the answer is a definite "Yes!" Increased dexterity with this technology has boosted librarians' confidence, invigorating them with an exciting new skill. Experience with a broader range of reference queries has enhanced research expertise, Windows competence, and Internet proficiency. Project participation has opened the door to developing new and effective teaching strategies to reach faculty, students, staff, and remote users–and perhaps even librarian colleagues–in the foreseeable future. Having a finger on the pulse of the general public and its information needs has also provided input for improving other university resources. Through Q and A NJ participation, first-hand data on consumer health concerns has resulted in the addition and expansion of UMDNJ's HealthyNJ consumer health Web site at <http://www.healthynj.org/>. Food-for-thought for future projects has been gathered, and our imaginations have been stimulated by the possibilities of interactive chat. Expansion of current UMDNJ participation is also a viable possibility as the project grows; perhaps a separate queue for health and medical questions will be established. Q and A NJ participation has also further strengthened collegial relationships, fortifying New Jersey's powerful library network. The Q and A NJ experience has been undeniably positive, and HSL@S librarians feel lucky to have been presented with this opportunity. Staff members are gratified by the feeling that the library made the right decision to participate, and proud of the success of a multi-type library project of this scale. We are excited about the future and the potential of Q and A NJ.

Ask a Librarian Virtual Reference Services at the Boeing Library

Julie Martin

SUMMARY. For the last five years, the Library Services organization in The Boeing Company has seen trends common to most corporate libraries. The number of people visiting physical library locations has declined significantly, and the number of people accessing library Web sites and using the Internet to find information has grown enormously. With these trends firmly in mind, the Library Services organization began looking for ways to reach customers who were growing more and more accustomed to working in a virtual environment. The organization's research with the corporate search engine group showed that people searching the Boeing intranet and the Internet have significant frustrations in finding what they need. Library Services viewed this as an opportunity to use the unique skills of librarians to help meet customer needs at the point of their greatest frustration: inadequate search results. The solution was Ask a Librarian, a virtual reference service linked to the corporate search engine. This article describes the steps that led to the implementation of Ask a Librarian, how the service works, the benefits of its use, and the challenges the Library Services organization faces as it continues to improve the service. *[Article copies available for a fee from The Haworth Document Delivery Service: 1-800-HAWORTH. E-mail address: <docdelivery@haworthpress.com> Website: <http://www.HaworthPress.com> © 2003 by The Haworth Press, Inc. All rights reserved.]*

Julie Martin has worked for Boeing for six years on a number of projects related to digital library development, information filtering, taxonomy and metadata schemas, and virtual reference services.

[Haworth co-indexing entry note]: "Ask a Librarian Virtual Reference Services at the Boeing Library." Martin, Julie. Co-published simultaneously in *Internet Reference Services Quarterly* (The Haworth Information Press, an imprint of The Haworth Press, Inc.) Vol. 8, No. 1/2, 2003, pp. 127-135; and: *Virtual Reference Services: Issues and Trends* (ed: Stacey Kimmel, and Jennifer Heise) The Haworth Information Press, an imprint of The Haworth Press, Inc., 2003, pp. 127-135. Single or multiple copies of this article are available for a fee from The Haworth Document Delivery Service [1-800-HAWORTH, 9:00 a.m. - 5:00 p.m. (EST). E-mail address: docdelivery@haworthpress.com].

10.1300/J136v08n01_11

KEYWORDS. Virtual reference, digital reference, chat software, special libraries, corporate libraries

INTRODUCTION

For the last five years, the Library Services organization in The Boeing Company has seen trends common to most corporate libraries. Personal contact with users has diminished since the library began providing Web-based access to the library catalog and other electronic collections. Research and reference requests have also declined significantly as users turn to the Internet, the Boeing intranet, and the Library Services Web site for their information needs. Library staff knew from working with the corporate search engine group that users are frequently frustrated with the results of their searches. They have difficulty locating the information they need and don't know where to turn when their queries result in too much, too little, or the wrong information. Viewing this as an opportunity to promote library services, and recognizing that librarians are uniquely suited to helping people find information, the library services staff developed a plan to integrate reference services with the corporate search engine.

The Birth of an Idea

Boeing Library Services has a long history of providing digital reference services. Library Services has offered e-mail reference services since the company first started providing desktop access, and when the Internet arrived, a Web form was added for submitting research and reference requests. As staff contemplated integrating reference services with the search engine, one idea was to put a link from the enterprise search site to the research request form. Further brainstorming led to the idea of using chat room software to develop a virtual reference desk. Without realizing it, library staff had stumbled across one of the hottest trends in library reference services.

Getting Started

When the project started, the team members weren't aware of the research on virtual reference services under way in the field. This may have been an oversight or simply that the library was on the leading edge of a trend that hadn't yet exploded into general awareness. The project team spent about a month defining staffing arrangements and experimenting with software to determine the requirements for the Library Services organization.

Because staff would handle chat requests along with other duties, a key requirement would be sound–an auditory signal to alert the staff when a customer enters the chat room. A Web-based product with a customizable interface was desired; in addition, the software would need to be hosted on Boeing's server behind a firewall. The Library Services organization chose ChatSpace, a product already used in the company, because it met these criteria. In June 2000, a two-week proof-of-concept trial began, using a free version of the basic product.

The trial would be customers' first look at Ask a Librarian, a virtual reference desk linked from the corporate search engine, where librarians offer live help and quick, thorough answers to customer questions.

Early Experiences–Librarian Bots or Human Search Engines?

Library services did not advertise Ask a Librarian before beginning the trial, so Boeing customers' first exposure to it was through a note and button that popped up at the bottom of their search results screen. The trial resulted in interesting experiments and questions from customers, as shown in the transcripts (see Table 1).

While this isn't recommended as a marketing tactic, the service did get a lot of exposure to new customers one day when the search engine failed. For several hours, all searches on the corporate search engine returned no hits and directed customers to the Ask a Librarian service. As users poured into the chat room, confused and upset that they suddenly could no longer find anything, staff scrambled to explain the situation and to help them locate information through other channels. It was a great opportunity to introduce customers to the resourcefulness of librarians!

The Lure of Anonymity

It was apparent early on that Boeing customers liked to be anonymous. Although the system prompted them to enter their names when they logged in to Ask a Librarian, every customer used the default user name, *guest*, instead. A number was added to the guest's name if more than one entered, but it was confusing for librarians and users to identify who was online.

To remedy the situation, the *guest* default was removed and the text changed to request that users enter a nickname. This solution allowed them to remain anonymous and gave staff a way to differentiate the customers.

TABLE 1. Transcript of a Chat Session

LibrarianVicki	Can we help you?
Guest36	sateliteobit
LibrarianVicki	Do you need an orbit on a particular satellite?
Guest36	yes
LibrarianVicki	Can you tell me which one?
Guest36	no
LibrarianVicki	What specifically are you looking for?
Guest36	orbitingsatelites
LibrarianVicki	Without more information, I don't know what I can do.
LibrarianVicki	I do know that the Kent Library has some books on satellite orbits.
Guest36	showmaps
LibrarianVicki	You can call them at 253-773-0590.
Guest36	wantvisual
Guest36	yes
LibrarianVicki	Are you looking for a website?
Guest36	yes
LibrarianVicki	I'll need to look for some.
LibrarianVicki	Can you give me your name and phone number so I can get back to you?
Guest27	Are the LibrariansRuth and Vicki bots?
LibrarianVicki	No, we're flesh and blood.
Guest27	oh . . . . . I see!
LibrarianVicki	To work this, all you have to do is type your request. We'll then try to find your information.
Guest27	Oh I see
Guest27	Cool
Guest27	I am looking for books about cultural etequette(sp) . . . . .
Guest27	. . . like if I travel to China . . . . what are the cultural rules I need to observe(?)
LibrarianVicki	We have some in our library here. What area of the country (Boeing site) are you in?
Guest27	I'm in Seattle . . . Renton
LibrarianVicki	Do you want me to email you a list of books, or would you rather check our catalog yourself?
Guest27	I'll try the catalog first. Then come back . . . . . is that ok?
LibrarianVicki	Sure. Our website is http://infoplus.boeing.com/
Guest27	Oh thanks . . . . I'll check it out . . . . . Hope I didn't offend you with my 'bot' question.
LibrarianVicki	Not at all.
Guest27	This is a really oool idea . . . . . check you later!
LibrarianVicki	btw here are the urls for cultural info via the library reading room http://www.craighead.com/intranet/company.ihtml?companyid=58943203 and http://www-library.boeing.com/interacts/

HOW IT WORKS–TACTICS, TOOLS, AND TRENDS

Staffing

The Ask a Librarian service is staffed Monday through Friday from 6:00 a.m. to 4:00 p.m. by the major regional libraries in Boeing: Arizona, Puget Sound, Southern California, and Missouri. Each region establishes its own schedule. About thirty-five librarians staff the service each week. The service works best when at least two librarians in proximity are on duty; generally, one librarian is the primary contact, and the other serves as a backup if the load increases.

Roles and Responsibilities

Ask a Librarian focal point contacts have been designated in each region. The contacts have two roles. First, they answer region-specific questions. Second, they help to resolve scheduling problems.

Training

To prepare the library staff for offering virtual reference services, the Library Services organization created a set of guidelines and best practices, a resource guide to the most frequently used resources, and a Web site with links to these materials. The Web site also has software tips, contact information, transcripts, metrics, and research on digital reference services. New staff members are encouraged to become familiar with the software during off hours, and they are paired with experienced staff members until they feel comfortable in the environment.

Library Services' Virtual Reference Service Guidelines

The Library Services organization created these guidelines for staff who provide chat services:

1. Chat reference works best when the customer's question can be answered on the spot. Look at the question and determine whether you have a reasonable chance of finding the answer quickly. A quick list of URLs is available in the chat application and, if the answer isn't there, it can often be found with a quick search of the Boeing intranet.
2. If you are going to perform a search, let the customer know that you may need a few minutes. Then use the five-minute rule: If you haven't made

progress in finding the answer in five minutes, get the customer's name and e-mail address or phone number to contact them later.

3. If the question appears complex, it is appropriate to ask immediately for a name and e-mail address or phone number.

4. Some questions obviously belong to a specific region. When you get a question that should be answered by another region, ask for the customer's name and e-mail address or phone number, and let the customer know that someone will answer his or her question. Then forward the question and contact information by e-mail to the Ask a Librarian focal point in the appropriate region. It is the responsibility of the regional focal point to respond to the customer.

Software

The Community Server 2.1 product from Akiva (formerly ChatSpace) is used to provide the Ask a Librarian service. This software has a number of features that met the Library Service organization's initial system criteria and requirements:

- Java applet–no client or plug-ins to install
- Installed on the Boeing server rather than on vendor's
- Sound for alerting moderator
- Customizable interface
- Moderated chat room
- Private person-to-person chat–useful for collaboration between librarians
- Records transcripts in Jet database or SQL

In the next year, the software will be upgraded to a product with more contact center functionality, such as queuing, separate windows for each interaction, the ability to send a copy of the session transcript to the customer, and the ability to add locally assigned metadata to the transcripts in the database.

While there has been an emphasis on co-browsing functionality in chat reference software, this feature may be more useful as a separate training tool than as part of the chat interaction. Boeing customers are busy, and while some may be interested in learning how to perform a complex database search, most want either an immediate answer, or for staff to do the research offline and get back to them. Co-browsing technology is being considered for providing a one-on-one training service that users could schedule at their convenience.

Usage Trends

Usage over the past two years has been consistent, averaging between 15 and 20 questions a day, with the heaviest use occurring between 8:00 a.m. to 3:00 p.m.

Types of Questions

Some of the most frequent questions are requests for help locating Boeing documents, military and industry standards, Boeing policies and procedures, and business forms. Other common inquiries include requests for specific books or journal articles, human resources and benefits information, and software problems. While most questions are work related, staff members occasionally receive questions of a more personal nature. Depending on the questions, librarians are free to answer them at their own discretion.

FEEDBACK AND BENEFITS

User Feedback

Customer feedback has been tremendously positive. They frequently comment that they had been searching the intranet unsuccessfully for quite some time before they contacted the library. Even when the librarian is unsuccessful in answering their questions, they are very grateful for the help. It adds a wonderfully human element to what often can feel like an impersonal environment.

Staff Reactions

Not only has this service proved popular with Boeing customers, but the library staff members have benefited as well. They enjoy more contact with customers, better communication with Boeing librarians in other regions, and more familiarity with the resources and programs available in those regions. Boeing has merged with four companies in the past five years, and this sharing of regional knowledge has proved invaluable. They also think it's a lot of fun!

Service Improvements

Another benefit of this service is an increased awareness of customers' information needs. Staff members were able to use information from Ask a Librarian customers to improve other areas of the library organization. For example, an analysis of the chat room transcripts revealed that the most frequent requests were for help locating internal Boeing documents and, since there was no central location for these documents on the Boeing intranet, the library services organization developed a new section on the Library Services web site that provides a "one-stop-shop" for these important documents.

ISSUES AND CHALLENGES

Skills Required

A virtual reference service is a fast-paced environment requiring agility and flexibility. Staff members must have strong keyboarding skills and be comfortable multitasking. They must be able to quickly focus the customer's question, be familiar with Boeing jargon and, of course, have a thorough knowledge of the resources available in library databases, the Boeing intranet, and the external Web.

Evaluating Quality of Service

Evaluating quality of service is a sensitive issue to library managers and staff members. Traditional reference services have often been considered as much an art as a science. Digital reference software creates a transcript of that interaction that is now visible to managers and peers, and this makes many librarians uncomfortable. Not only is their performance more visible now, but the medium is less forgiving of mistakes. There are fewer cues to help determine the customer's questions. Customers expect more rapid responses than in a face-to-face interaction, and there are quirks in the way the software functions that can confuse the customer.

While training and experience may address some of these issues, other issues may be resolved through improvements in the software. The current software provides a basic chat room that allows multiple users and librarians to interact simultaneously. While usage is low enough that this generally isn't a problem, it can lead to confusion when things get busy. At times, customers answer one another's questions—which isn't necessarily a bad thing! Not only is this an issue for the librarians, but it also affects the quality of the transcripts.

While staff members have been creative in adapting to this environment, a real improvement will be to move to a product that provides queuing functionality so that staff can interact one-on-one with customers, and so that interactions can be captured as separate sessions in the transcript database. A future goal for Ask a Librarian is to develop a knowledge base of frequently asked questions from the transcripts. This effort will be significantly easier once the software is upgraded.

Measuring Customer Satisfaction

Although anecdotal information indicates that Boeing customers find the service very helpful, formal procedures for gathering customer satisfaction metrics have not been implemented. This is an area to address as the Library Services organization moves forward with the service.

CONCLUSION

The Library Services organization has been offering Ask a Librarian for two years, and it has become a standard part of library reference services. Staff members have grown comfortable working in the chat environment and have honed their skills in this form of communication. The decision to integrate the service with the enterprise search engine has led to increased visibility of corporate library services and has provided employees with somewhere to turn when their search efforts prove frustrating. While the Library Services organization will continue to improve search interfaces and electronic access to the library collections, this experience with virtual reference services has shown that there is indeed a place for flesh-and-blood librarians in the digital library and on the corporate intranet.

Managing Data Collection
for Real-Time Reference:
Lessons from the AskERIC Live! Experience

Yvonne Belanger
R. David Lankes
Pauline Lynch Shostack

SUMMARY. Successful management of a real-time digital reference service requires effective and efficient data collection to provide accurate and useful information about service processes and outcomes. This article describes the data collection procedures developed by AskERIC for its real-time reference service; in particular, this article will describe how these procedures address limitations, gaps, and inaccuracies in the data as passively captured by software. Finally, particular issues and considerations for service managers about various statistical measures within the real-time environment are discussed. *[Article copies available for a fee from The Haworth Document Delivery Service: 1-800-HAWORTH. E-mail address: <docdelivery@haworthpress.com> Website: <http://www.HaworthPress.com> © 2003 by The Haworth Press, Inc. All rights reserved.]*

Yvonne Belanger (yvonne@iis.syr.edu) is Project Manager for the Virtual Reference Desk Project and former AskERIC QA Project Manager; R. David Lankes (rdlankes@ericir.syr.edu) is Director of the Information Institute of Syracuse; and at the time of submission, Pauline Lynch Shostack (pauline@askeric.org) was the AskERIC Project Coordinator; all at the Information Institute of Syracuse, 621 Skytop Road, Suite 160, Syracuse, NY 13244.

The AskERIC Project is a sponsored program of Syracuse University funded by the U.S. Department of Education.

[Haworth co-indexing entry note]: "Managing Data Collection for Real-Time Reference: Lessons from the AskERIC Live! Experience." Belanger, Yvonne, R. David Lankes, and Pauline Lynch Shostack. Co-published simultaneously in *Internet Reference Services Quarterly* (The Haworth Information Press, an imprint of The Haworth Press, Inc.) Vol. 8, No. 1/2, 2003, pp. 137-148; and: *Virtual Reference Services: Issues and Trends* (ed: Stacey Kimmel, and Jennifer Heise) The Haworth Information Press, an imprint of The Haworth Press, Inc., 2003, pp. 137-148. Single or multiple copies of this article are available for a fee from The Haworth Document Delivery Service [1-800-HAWORTH, 9:00 a.m. - 5:00 p.m. (EST). E-mail address: docdelivery@haworthpress.com].

KEYWORDS. Virtual reference, digital reference services, statistics, evaluation, real-time reference, AskERIC Live!

INTRODUCTION

Successful management of a real-time digital reference service requires effective and efficient data collection to provide accurate and useful information about service processes and outcomes. Any library or AskA service contemplating the launch of or seeking to evaluate a virtual reference service is faced with a number of questions of what statistics are useful to capture, and how to go about capturing these statistics. The following description of the procedures developed by the AskERIC service[1] illustrates some of the challenges and considerations facing managers of virtual reference services and outlines methods for and suggestions for how and why to capture certain information about the service. Finally, future improvements that would support the development and management of quality digital reference services are discussed.

THE AskERIC Live! SERVICE

Since November 1992, AskERIC has provided digital reference services via e-mail to over 250,000 parents, teachers, policymakers, and educators. For several years AskERIC contemplated and planned the addition of a real-time reference service to complement the services and resources currently offered. After a series of pilots, AskERIC Live! was launched in October 2001.[2] From October 2001 to June 2002, AskERIC Live! conducted over 1,100 real-time reference transactions.

General Service Characteristics

AskERIC Live! assists patrons with questions about educational theory and practice; the majority of patrons of the service (62%) are provided assistance by means of the ERIC database or the resources available on either the AskERIC Web site or another ERIC Clearinghouse's Web site. AskERIC Live! uses 24/7 Reference software. 24/7 Reference is a project of the Metropolitan Cooperative Library System (MCLS), supported by Federal LSTA funding and administered by the California State Library.[3] Currently offered three hours each weekday afternoon (1:00 p.m. to 4:00 p.m. Eastern time), the volume for the service averages three sessions per hour during available hours, with a mean weekly volume of approximately 40 sessions per week for the period of January to May 2002, a volume that represents approximately 5% of the total volume of digital reference handled by the AskERIC service.

In keeping with the distributed service model of AskERIC's successful e-mail reference service, patrons are assisted by AskERIC Central staff members at the ERIC Clearinghouse on Information and Technology, as well as by librarians and subject specialists at other participating ERIC Clearinghouses around the country. The same AskERIC Central personnel that manage AskERIC's e-mail reference service act as administrators for the real-time service. As a participant in the 24/7 Reference network, AskERIC also has the ability to transfer patrons with queries outside the scope of the AskERIC service to public librarians participating in the 24/7 Reference consortium.

Data Collection: Informal Needs Assessment

In addition to policy development and staff training, an important goal of the initial pilot tests of the AskERIC Live! service was to determine how to gather data about the new service, and then to evaluate the extent to which the automated statistical reports available from the software could gather and report this data accurately and effectively. During these pilots, it quickly became apparent that regardless of which software package was selected for the service, additional procedures would need to be implemented to collect data beyond that automatically recorded and reported by the software. The following section discusses some of the inherent limitations of the automated reporting and describes AskERIC's procedures for the collection of meaningful, useful, and accurate data about the service.

DATA COLLECTION PROCEDURES: A TWO-FOLD APPROACH

The data collection strategy used by AskERIC is based upon three primary service management considerations: ease of collection, reliability, and utility. In order to fully and accurately gather all of the information needed about the service, AskERIC employs two separate instruments: a detailed Web-based transaction log form, and an Excel workbook containing general statistics as recorded by the shift administrator. These two mechanisms serve different purposes, are simple to use, and provide a significant amount of useful and reliable information beyond what the 24/7 software provides. Some of the information recorded is redundantly collected by the software as well (e.g., was the patron's Web browser limited in its ability to fully utilize the software's interactive capabilities?); however, it has proven to be much simpler and less time consuming to actively collect this data using a radio button on the Web form log rather than to conduct analysis of the transaction logs at a later date. Continuous data collection has some definite advantages in terms of gathering a large sample size of data for analysis as well as avoiding the difficulty of determining a sampling procedure or defining a "typical" time period for a nascent service, and has been advocated for effectively monitoring, managing and improving the quality of reference services.[4]

Instrument #1: Web-Based Log Form

Upon completion of the transaction, the AskERIC staff member uses a Web-based log form to report session-level statistics (see Figure 1). The log form writes this session-level information to an Access database for later synthesis and analysis. To support aggregation of information about the service at various units of analysis, the form includes space for the librarian's name, ERIC clearinghouse affiliation, and date of session (preset by default with today's date). Information is recorded about session length, technical information, whether or not a follow-up was required or problems encountered, and type of assistance provided. The form also provides a structure for content analysis of the session, including the AskERIC controlled vocabulary as well as additional descriptive keywords. Finally, this log form provides free text space so that staff can record any issues or problems encountered during the session. Despite the amount of detail collected about each session, this form takes only a minute or two to fill out and is not considered burdensome by the AskERIC staff. Using a browser that supports auto-fill of fields speeds data entry, as do typical Web form features such as radio buttons, check-boxes and drop-down menus.

Instrument #2: Administrator Spreadsheet

In addition to the session-level information recorded by librarians using the Web-based log form, the administrator for each shift uses a simple Excel spreadsheet for daily recording. The shift administrator keeps a count of sessions per librarian, with sessions transferred to the 24/7 Reference network counted separately from sessions completed by AskERIC staff. Although the software obviously can also provide a count of the number of sessions per librarian, the difficulties with this statistic as recorded by the software will be discussed in the next section. In addition, the administrator notes the number of hours of service in order to provide a context for interpretation of other measures of service volume. It is also helpful to include commentary about any unusual incidents during that shift that may have affected the hours of service, e.g., severe network problems or a shortened shift due to a holiday closing. In

FIGURE 1. AskERIC Live! Log Form

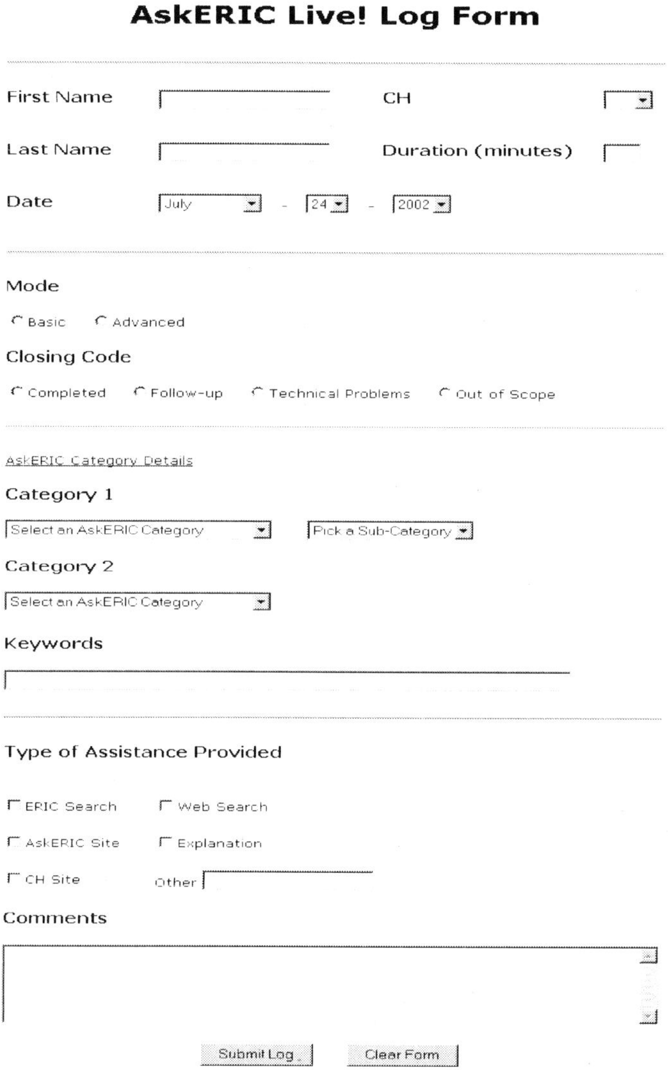

AskERIC Live! Log Form

First Name [   ]   CH   [▾]

Last Name [   ]   Duration (minutes) [   ]

Date   [July   ▾] - [24 ▾] - [2002 ▾]

Mode

○ Basic   ○ Advanced

Closing Code

○ Completed   ○ Follow-up   ○ Technical Problems   ○ Out of Scope

AskERIC Category Details

Category 1

[Select an AskERIC Category   ▾]   [Pick a Sub-Category ▾]

Category 2

[Select an AskERIC Category   ▾]

Keywords

[   ]

Type of Assistance Provided

☐ ERIC Search   ☐ Web Search

☐ AskERIC Site   ☐ Explanation

☐ CH Site   Other [   ]

Comments

[   ]

[Submit Log]   [Clear Form]

order to balance workload volume from the e-mail reference service with time spent on the virtual reference desk, the administrator records the number of hours spent by staff at other clearinghouses "staffing" the real-time desk. Finally, patrons may access the AskERIC Live! service from any one of five locations on the AskERIC Web site; the referring URL as patrons enter the AskERIC Live! queue is noted to provide a final piece of context for service volume numbers. Because more than one access point is provided, this information offers not only insight into which links are most effective in attracting patrons to the service, but information about the point at which patrons seek assistance in navigating resources on the AskERIC Web site.[5]

CHALLENGES TO ACCURATE DATA COLLECTION

Within the context of managing a virtual reference service, there are issues inherent to the real-time service delivery mode that present significant challenges for accurate data collection. Several statistics are either not captured at all or not measured accurately by the software used by AskERIC; limitations exists in other software products currently in use for real-time reference.[6] Table 1 offers a side-by-side comparison of the statistics captured by AskERIC using their Web-based session log form and the administrator's Excel spreadsheet, along with an indication of whether or not the software captures that information, and some commentary regarding each measure. Service managers attempting to decide what kind of information to collect may find this information helpful in determining the usefulness of some of these service measures.

Below is an elaboration of a few of the issues and challenges in accurately capturing statistics in an accurate and meaningful way, along with the rationales behind some of the solutions implemented by the AskERIC service to address these difficulties.

Number of Sessions

Many software products used for real-time reference, especially those built from commercial Web contact center software such as 24/7, collect and report statistics regarding the number of real-time sessions per librarian over any specified time period. However, AskERIC has found it to be more useful to collect this statistic separately, because the numbers of sessions reported by the software logs frequently do not reflect the true number of reference transactions. Users may become temporarily disconnected yet quickly reconnect and continue the session; although the software would judge this to represent two separate sessions, it seems clear this situation represents only one refer-

TABLE 1. Statistics Collected

Descriptive Statistic	Collected within software?	Collected by AskERIC?	Explanation
Session length	Service Time or Handle Time	Yes–Web session log form	Problems with accuracy– see discussion below.
Number of reference transactions	Number of Sessions or Calls Handled	Yes–Administrator shift spreadsheet	Problems with accuracy– see discussion below.
Number of patrons transferred to 24/7 network	Calls Handled With Transfer To or Transfer From	Yes–Administrator shift spreadsheet	Ease and simplicity of accurate manual collection
Number of hours of service	No	Yes–Administrator shift spreadsheet	Provides important context for service volume data
Narrative comments about session by librarian	No	Yes–Web session log form	Encourages staff to report problems and actively contribute ideas about service development and quality improvement of service delivery
Patron browser capability ("Basic" or "Advanced" mode)	Yes	Yes–Web session log form	Determines what mode of interaction should be emphasized during librarian training
Topic of patron question according to AskERIC controlled vocabulary	No	Yes–Web session log form	Software does not currently support the use of rich vocabularies for content analysis
Additional topic keywords describing session	No	Yes–Web session log form	Supports better content analysis and information for vocabulary development efforts
Resources used during session	Transcript, including URLs visited	Yes–Web session log form	Checkbox on session log form is simpler than manually mining stored transcripts; Integrated data mining tools could support automated transcript analysis
ERIC Clearinghouse affiliation of AskERIC staff member	No	Yes–Web session log form	Allows for aggregation of statistics by service unit (ERIC Clearinghouse)
Patron wait time before connecting with librarian	Average Queue Time	No	AskERIC can bring on additional staff to handle excess load; wait time is not currently a concern

ence transaction. Recent improvements to the eGain software underlying the 24/7 Reference product have improved the software's ability to accurately count transferred sessions, but the ability to connect the pieces of an interrupted transaction is still lacking.

From a management perspective, the minimal burden of maintaining a simple tally of the true number of sessions per librarian and overall number of patrons served is less of a concern than the more problematic lack of accurate information about such a fundamental measure of service volume. Measuring the number of transactions in this way ensures that only complete exchanges are counted, and that multiple counts are not recorded for the same transaction.[7]

Session Length

One of the most useful pieces of information about service processes from a management perspective may be session length (defined here as the amount of elapsed time between making the initial connection with the patron and closing the session). As measured by AskERIC staff using the Web-based session log form, the average session (service-wide) lasts 16 minutes. Accurate information about average session lengths, as well as outlier session lengths, supports decision-making about staffing and scheduling, provides information about staff workload, and informs policy development. It would be interesting to learn whether patterns exist in session lengths, and whether they are consistent within and across various digital reference organizations, but these kinds of comparisons can only be made if the data are collected in a consistent and reliable manner.

For a number of reasons, "session length" or "handle time" as reported by the software is not reliable. A variety of ordinary situations create discrepancies between the session length as recorded by the software and the "reality" of session length as experienced by the librarian and patron. As mentioned above, the capability to transfer patrons between librarians and between consortium partners is a valuable feature, but one which has historically caused problems in the accurate measurement of session lengths. For example, the version of the 24/7 Reference software initially used by AskERIC Live! would record a twenty minute transaction for both Librarian A and Librarian B in a scenario where Librarian A spent five minutes negotiating a query with a patron before transferring them to Subject Expert B for a fifteen minute exchange. Recent software improvements include more accurate logging of transferred sessions and have therefore improved the ability of the software to correctly measure the actual time spent with the patron in this kind of scenario. However, additional improvements are still needed in this area. Inaccurate session lengths are frequently recorded when patrons disconnect prior to the mutually agreed upon conclusion of the reference interaction, either due to technical problems in establishing a connection or the familiar virtual reference phenomenon of the "disappearing patron."[8] Sessions that are not properly closed due to librarian error or technical problems may also result in passively recorded session lengths that are clearly not accurate. AskERIC has found it more efficient to simply have librarians record the information upon conclusion of a session rather than struggle with cleaning up the data as recorded by the software to filter out or remove the invalid or inaccurate session lengths recorded.

OTHER MANAGEMENT CONSIDERATIONS FOR DATA COLLECTION

Staff Support

To maintain their support for data collection efforts, managers should keep reference staff informed of the planned use of any statistics they are asked to collect.[9] AskERIC staff members are actively involved in the ongoing development of the log form and the uses of the information collected, and are encouraged to provide feedback about the questions and options included on the log form.

Potential Uses of Collected Data

Methods for assessing and improving digital reference services are beginning to emerge. McClure et al. have created a scheme for measuring and evaluating digital reference services that advocates data collection in up to four areas for use in benchmarking and standards development: outcome measures (quality of answers); process measures (effectiveness and efficiency); economic measures; and user satisfaction.[10] AskERIC's statistical data collection procedures address a significant number of outcome and process measures. In addition, AskERIC's attention to the accuracy of data collected on the amount of staff time spent on the service can also provide the groundwork for future economic analysis of the service. In order to address outcome and user satisfaction measures in service evaluation, AskERIC also utilizes periodic pop-up point of use surveys and employs transcript reviews.

Even without the richer information available in user surveys or reference transcripts, the simple statistics collected by the Web session log form can be potentially useful for policy development or quality improvement efforts. For instance, Figure 2 represents a thought-provoking comparison between average session length and the frequency of the need for follow-up via email after the real-time transaction for seven staff members.

In-depth analysis could verify the existence or strength of a correlation between session length and frequency of follow-up. However, from a service management point of view, even the simple comparison shown here may be useful for quality improvement in a number of ways. Service managers can use

FIGURE 2. Duration of Sessions

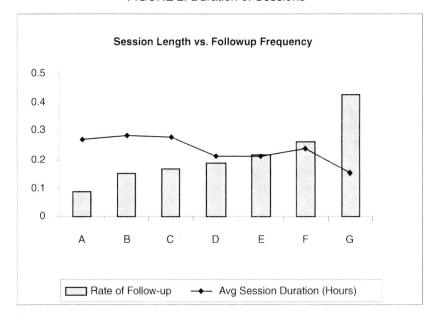

this type of information to launch a discussion among personnel of service goals and policies; some services might aim to reduce the need for follow-up, while others might wish to reduce the average session length. Managers might also use this type of information to gain insight into the true amount of staff time typically required to completely assist digital reference patrons. Finally, managers could even consider the comparison between session length and staff time on an individual level to investigate the impact of particular staff development programs (e.g., training on Web searching techniques). Ideally, software and data collection tools would support combining this information with patron satisfaction data obtained from formal surveys or aggregated unsolicited, to combine process-oriented measures with outcome-oriented measures. As services grow and mature, the range and sophistication of their data collection efforts should also develop.[11]

CONCLUSION

Lankes, Gross, and McClure note that digital reference practitioners and the vendors who serve them must pursue ways to integrate and embed quality standards and assessment data into the processes, software, and infrastructure of digital reference.[12] The development of processes and procedures for embedding ongoing assessment and evaluation into digital reference services is a challenging yet essential task.

For the virtual reference service manager, reliable and detailed statistics about service performance can be a valuable tool in gaining insight into areas for policy development or improvement of service delivery. The data collection procedures AskERIC has put in place for their real-time service address process measures and provide support for economic analysis of the service. In the case of AskERIC as well as other services, software tools must support comparing and cross-referencing service performance data, such as the type captured by AskERIC's Web-based session log form, with other richer forms of data available, such as transcripts and user surveys. Digital reference service providers as well as software developers must do more work to create and develop tools to support innovative strategies for collecting reliable and useful data about digital reference services.

NOTES

1. AskERIC Web site. Available: <http://askeric.org/>.

2. AskERIC Live! Available: <http://askeric.org/QA/userform.shtml>.

3. 24/7 Reference. Available: <http://www.247ref.org/>.

4. R. Aluri, "Improving Reference Service: The Case for Using a Continuous Quality Improvement Method," *RQ* 33, no.2 (1994): 220-236.

5. The AskERIC Web site logs an average of 6 million hits (90,000 unique visitors); to keep service traffic in line with current service capacity, links are distributed among pages which receive relatively moderate rather than heavy traffic.

6. For a further discussion of the functionality and limitations of software products used for real-time reference, see S. Coffman, "We'll Take It From Here: Further Developments We'd Like to See in Virtual Reference Software," *Information Technology and Libraries* 20, no. 3 (September 2001): 149-53.

7. J. Bertot, C.R. McClure, and J. Ryan. *Statistics and Performance Measures for Public Library Networked Services.* (Chicago: American Library Association, 2000): 12.

8. Matt Marsteller and Paul Neuhaus, "The Chat Reference Experience at Carnegie Mellon University." (2001). Available: <http://www.contrib.andrew.cmu.edu/~matthewm/ALA_2001_chat.html>. Accessed: July 11, 2002.

9. H. White, "Measurement at the Reference Desk," *Drexel Library Quarterly* 17(1), 3-35.

10. C.R. McClure and R.D. Lankes, "Assessing Quality in Digital Reference Services: A Research Prospectus." (2001). Available: <http://quartz.syr.edu/quality/Overview.htm>. Accessed: July 15, 2002.

11. C.R. McClure, R.D.Lankes, M. Gross, and B. Choltco-Devlin, *Statistics, Measures, and Quality Standards for Assessing Digital Reference Library Services: Guidelines and Procedures.* 2002.

12. R.D. Lankes, C.R. McClure, and M. Gross, "Cost, Statistics, Measures, and Standards for Digital Reference Services: A Preliminary View," *Library Trends* 51, no. 3 (2003): Forthcoming.

Exploring the Synchronous Digital Reference Interaction for Query Types, Question Negotiation, and Patron Response

Matthew R. Marsteller
Danianne Mizzy

SUMMARY. The authors explored synchronous digital reference transcripts, using the first full year of *Chat* reference data from Carnegie Mellon University. Synchronous digital reference transcripts are the text of the interchange between the librarian and the patron when they converse using chat software via the Internet. The article is focused on three stages of the synchronous digital reference interaction. The first stage is the query posed by the patron, the second stage is the questioning employed by the librarian in response to the patron's query, and the third stage is the patron's response to the librarian's questioning. Results indicate that reference interviews occurred 64% of the time with an over-

Matthew R. Marsteller (matthewm@andrew.cmu.edu) is Physics and Math Librarian, Engineering and Science Library, Room 4400, Wean Hall, Carnegie Mellon University, Pittsburgh, PA 15213-3890. Danianne Mizzy (danianne@pitt.edu) is Public Service Librarian, Hillman Library, University of Pittsburgh, G-22 Hillman Library, University of Pittsburgh, Pittsburgh, PA 15260.

The authors would like to recognize the invaluable assistance of Elaine Rubenstein of the University of Pittsburgh's Office of Measurement and Evaluation of Teaching. Her work and advice on the statistical analysis was deeply appreciated.

[Haworth co-indexing entry note]: "Exploring the Synchronous Digital Reference Interaction for Query Types, Question Negotiation, and Patron Response." Marsteller, Matthew R., and Danianne Mizzy. Co-published simultaneously in *Internet Reference Services Quarterly* (The Haworth Information Press, an imprint of The Haworth Press, Inc.) Vol. 8, No. 1/2, 2003, pp. 149-165; and: *Virtual Reference Services: Issues and Trends* (ed: Stacey Kimmel, and Jennifer Heise) The Haworth Information Press, an imprint of The Haworth Press, Inc., 2003, pp. 149-165. Single or multiple copies of this article are available for a fee from The Haworth Document Delivery Service [1-800-HAWORTH, 9:00 a.m. - 5:00 p.m. (EST). E-mail address: docdelivery@haworthpress.com].

10.1300/J136v08n01_13

whelmingly positive response by the patron. Negative responses occurred in just five of 425 transcripts. Patron query types were similar to those found in a traditional reference setting. *[Article copies available for a fee from The Haworth Document Delivery Service: 1-800-HAWORTH. E-mail address: <docdelivery@haworthpress.com> Website: <http://www.HaworthPress.com> © 2003 by The Haworth Press, Inc. All rights reserved.]*

KEYWORDS. Reference interview, digital reference, chat reference, virtual reference, synchronous, real-time reference, question negotiation, open ended questioning, case study

INTRODUCTION

Understanding the synchronous digital reference interaction is important because more and more libraries are choosing to serve remote patrons in this fashion. The authors use the term "interaction" advisedly because many librarians and researchers question whether the reference interview is necessary, appropriate, or even possible in the digital reference environment. This study examines different facets of this question by analyzing transcripts of the *Carnegie Mellon University Chat* (hereafter *Chat*) reference service.

For the purpose of the study, the reference interview is defined as librarians employing open or closed questions[1] to probe and clarify patron queries. This definition follows that used by Ross and Nilsen.[2] For clarity, question will always refer to the librarian's interrogative and query to the patron's interrogative. However, since not all patron queries necessitate a reference interview ("What are the library's hours?" being a classic example), it naturally follows that the type of query posed by the patron needs to be categorized. This categorization allows the authors to look for relationships between the complexity of a patron's initial query and the question style employed by the librarian in response. This also allows reporting as to the correctness of two prevailing perceptions about synchronous digital reference: (1) that patrons are only asking ready reference, factual-type queries and (2) that since a real reference interview is impossible, these are the only type of queries that the medium is suited to answering. The authors also explore the perception that synchronous digital reference patrons are in such a rush that they don't have the patience for a traditional reference interview. Therefore this study examines the patron's response to the librarian's response to see if the reaction to questioning by the librarian was favorable or unfavorable.

LITERATURE REVIEW

The above mentioned perceptions of synchronous digital reference interactions were discussed on two electronic mailing lists focused on digital reference, DIG_REF and livereference,[3] and in conversations with colleagues. However, the idea of a negative response to an extended patron/librarian exchange in e-mail reference was raised by Hahn[4] in 1997 and further elaborated by Sloan, when he stated that "both staff and users saw 'high dialogue penalties' (i.e., the decreasing usefulness of extended dialogues) as a major limitation."[5] In describing synchronous digital reference, Francoeur observed that librarians may feel "that the user has less commitment to the interaction than is appropriate and is uncooperative in participating in the back and forth of the reference interview."[6] He also observed that users "can be impatient and demanding during the chat, and in general help to create a reference encounter that feels more pressured than is typical at a reference desk."[7] Trump and Tuttle noted that librarians have reported "feeling (self-induced) pressure to answer questions quickly, sometimes at the expense of a better reference interview."[8] In the same vein, Marsteller and Neuhaus found that 60% of librarian "chat operators" believed that "[t]he chat operator's ability to guide the reference interaction" was "Worse" or "Much Worse" when comparing "Chat" to "In-person."[9] Smyth and Johnston neatly summed this up when they observed that librarians are "feeling pressure to perform at [the] speed of Google."[10]

The results reported by Janes in his survey of 648 public and academic reference librarians' attitudes towards digital reference are consistent with the observations above. (Please note that the survey did not distinguish between synchronous and asynchronous digital reference methods and that only a small percentage of survey respondents had actually used a synchronous method to receive or answer queries,[11] so perceptions were not based on experience of synchronous digital reference in most cases.) To the question of how well digital reference serves various kinds of questions, 80% responded that ready reference questions would be well served by digital reference services. Only 32.9% thought detailed research questions would be well served, and nearly half, 46.2%, thought detailed research questions would be poorly served.[12] Janes later observed that this "almost visceral reaction against research questions in digital reference is often tied to the nature of the interview, or the lack thereof, in this environment . . . "[13] Obviously, there is a strong perception that the digital medium is far better suited to assisting patrons with ready reference rather than detailed research questions.

Review of Patron Query Types

The authors looked to the literature to see if they could find a common categorization of query types asked by patrons in synchronous digital reference, but as Sears observed in her literature review, the "considerable amount of literature published on digital or electronic reference service . . . has dealt primarily with e-mail service."[14] Two published studies dealt specifically with synchronous digital reference. Sears' study of 153 questions drew on categories outlined by Katz,[15] but she ended up modifying this into: Reference Questions, subdivided into Ready-reference, Specific-search and Research questions; Policy & Procedural Questions, which contained two subdivisions; and Directional, which contained three subdivisions.[16] Kibbee, Ward, and Ma also examined synchronous interactions and used six categories to analyze 604 questions: Finding specific library materials, Information about UIUC library and services, Subject base [sic] research, Ready reference, Technical problem, and Questions about the service.[17] Other relevant though dissimilar typologies were found as part of conference presentations.[18] When the authors broadened the search to asynchronous digital reference, additional typologies were found.[19] It became clear that there was not one, common typology that would allow the comparison of the authors' results to that of other studies, so the authors designed their own. This design will be discussed in the methodology section.

Review of Librarian Question Types

In examining the librarian's response to the patron query, similar categories of no question (no interview), closed question, and open question were found to be widely employed to characterize the librarian's response to the patron's query.[20] Ross and Nilsen found that a reference interview employing closed or open questions during traditional face-to-face interactions was conducted only 51% and 48% of the time, respectively, in the two phases of their Library Visit study.[21] In a similar investigation, Dewdney and Ross found that "only 45% of the users in our study reported that they were asked one or more questions intended to elicit further information about their information need."[22] These studies established a baseline for how often reference interviews are conducted in traditional face-to-face interactions, and thus allowed the authors to compare the frequency of interviews that occurred in the case study.

Review of Patron Response Types

The authors were only able to find two studies that examined the patron's response to the librarian's use of open or closed questions. Auster and Lawton reported a correlation between user satisfaction with search results and the use of open or closed questions. Sessions using open questions received a slightly higher rating than sessions using closed questions for their 1983 study.[23] In their 1984 study they concluded that "interviews in which more open questions are asked result in searches in which users learn more and are more satisfied."[24]

METHODOLOGY

Three stages of the reference interaction were chosen for this analysis. The first stage was the query posed by the patron, the second stage was the questioning employed by the librarian in response to the patron's query, and the third stage was the patron's response to the librarian's questioning. The authors evaluated the transcripts that were available for study from the first year of operation of Carnegie Mellon's *Chat* service. The specific time period studied was from October of 2000 through September of 2001.

Background and Setting

Carnegie Mellon is a Research I institution located in Pittsburgh, Pennsylvania. The university has a student body of 7,500 students (2,500 graduate students) served by 3,000 faculty, research staff, and administrative staff. The *Chat* service serves the Carnegie Mellon community primarily, but the librarian will serve all who request help since there is no user authentication in place for the service. (A message on the Web page with the link to the service indicates that the service is intended only for the university community.) Carnegie Mellon Librarians and Information Assistants staff the service. Information Assistants are graduate students in the University of Pittsburgh MLIS program who are employed by Carnegie Mellon. The service is available Monday through Friday from 1:00 p.m. to 5:00 p.m. The software used for the service is LivePerson. Logs of the transactions are automatically captured by the software.

In light of the setting, it is important to note that this is just one case study and the reader must be cautioned not to generalize the results. The authors will draw comparisons with related or supporting studies in the statistical results.

Schema Development

As indicated in the literature review, the authors explored using schema from existing reference interaction research, but they found no standardization. The authors therefore decided to craft their own schema, or set of categories, that attempted to capture the nuances of digital reference. The schema (see Appendix A) included typical examples to better guide the authors in their analysis of the transcripts.

The schema was designed to allow for categorization into one of four levels of complexity for the Type of Patron Query. The four levels were (1) Directional/Policy/Procedure, (2) Known Item, (3) Facts/Ready Reference, and (4) Reference. In addition, many of the transcripts were coded for (5) Technical Problems or (6) Librarian Communications. Technical Problems for the Type of Patron Query were defined as a loss of (or failure in) communications before the patron could even pose their query. Librarian Communications included both internal and external messages. Internal messages were usually for shift turnover or for training of new personnel. External messages dealt with librarians at other institutions contacting Carnegie Mellon's service due to their curiosity about chat reference.

The categorization of the Librarian's Response was extremely straightforward because of the uniformity found in the literature. The categories were (1) No Question Asked, (2) Closed Question Asked, and (3) Open Question Asked. In addition, many of the transcripts were coded for (4) Technical Problems and (5) Librarian Communications. Technical Problems for the Librarian's Response were defined as a loss of (or failure in) communications after the patron had asked their query but before the librarian could respond, plus any earlier loss of communications. Librarian Communications identified the librarian's response to an internal or external librarian.

The typology for Patron's Response was designed to categorize the patron reaction to the librarian's questioning. The categories were (1) Favorable, (2) Unfavorable and (3) None/Not Applicable. A favorable response was defined as a continuation of communication by the patron, which demonstrated their willingness to continue the dialogue. Unfavorable responses were defined as those that exhibited impatience, anger, or rudeness. Unfavorable responses could also be characterized by the patron abruptly terminating the dialogue. The third category, None/Not Applicable, was reserved for when the librarian had asked no question or librarian communications had taken place at stage 2, or when there was a technical problem. It is important to note that the authors could tell from the LivePerson logs when a transaction was terminated due to a technical problem versus when one was terminated purposefully by a patron.

Additional Design Considerations

The authors considered whether to analyze at the reference question level or at the reference interaction level. Multiple queries from a patron or multiple responding questions from a librarian could occur in a single transaction. It was decided to make the unit of measure the reference interaction. Following a procedure similar to the one described by Ross and Nilsen,[25] the highest level of complexity present within each stage of the interaction would be used to categorize that entire stage. Thus, if a particular reference interaction contained both a directional query and a reference query, the reference interaction would be categorized using Reference Query for the Type of Patron Query. In a similar fashion, the presence of an open question would be used to characterize the librarian's response even if a number of closed questions were asked in the same interaction. For the Patron's Response to the librarian's questioning, any indication of a negative response to questioning would be used to categorize the interaction even if an indication of a positive response was also present.

Test for Interrater Reliability

Testing for interrater reliability was necessary because the set of transcripts were not going to be reviewed and coded by both authors (each author would review and code half). The mathematics underlying the test are described in a chapter of the *Handbook of Applied Multivariate Statistics and Mathematical Modeling*.[26] The authors chose to use at least 5% of the transcripts for the test. The transcripts were numbered sequentially and then an Internet random number generator was used to choose fifty numbers between 1 and 865.[27]

The authors independently evaluated all fifty randomly chosen transcripts using the schema as it was initially developed, and the results were compared to determine the level of agreement. The kappa, k, for the interrater agreement for the Type of Patron Query was .775, .770 for the Librarian's Response, and .62 for the Patron's Response. Most statisticians would consider that the first two measures of kappa demonstrated excellent agreement and the third demonstrated good agreement. This means that the agreement was good enough not to simply occur by chance. Next, the authors conferred about the transcripts that were in disagreement. This review allowed for refinement of the definitions and examples. These were then added to the schema definition (see Appendix A) so that the authors could achieve even greater agreement during the evaluation of the rest of the transcripts.

Data Compilation

Data were recorded in Microsoft Excel spreadsheets. Upon completion, the data were merged into a single file. A statistician with the University of Pittsburgh's Office of Measurement and Evaluation of Teaching worked with the authors to analyze the data with SPSS. The statistical results follow.

STATISTICAL RESULTS

Descriptive Statistics

As seen in Figure 1 below, the breakdown of the 865 transcripts by the Type of Patron Query included 143 (17%) Directional/Policy/Procedure queries, 123 (14%) Known Item queries, 86 (10%) Facts/Ready Reference queries, 85 (10%) Reference queries, 278 (32%) Technical Problems, and 150 (17%) Librarian Communications. Although the level of Technical Problems was a concern for the service, its only effect on the study was to reduce the sample size. The same was true of Librarian Communications.

Once the transcripts with Technical Problems and Librarian Communications were set aside, 425 transcripts remained where an exchange progressed through all three stages of the reference interaction. Figure 2 illustrates the breakdown of this subset of the transcripts. Although (1) Directional/Policy/Procedure queries formed the largest category, present in 141 transcripts (34%), the other categories were also well represented: (2) Known Item–120 transcripts (28%), (3) Facts/Ready Reference–82 transcripts (19%), and (4) Reference–82 transcripts (19%). It would appear, at least for Carnegie Mellon's service, the librarians must be prepared to handle more than just factual or ready reference questions.

These numbers appear to echo those of other studies, although the categories are slightly different, and the definitions of the categories differ some-

FIGURE 1. Breakdown of Patron Query Types (Sample Size = 865 Transcripts)

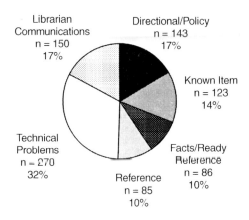

FIGURE 2. Type of Patron Query (425 Transcripts Where an Exchange Took Place)

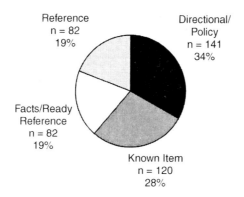

what. The Carnegie Mellon result of 34% for Directional/Policy/Procedural queries is between the 44.4% reported for Policy & Procedural plus Directional by Sears[28] and the 30.5% Library and services reported by Kibbee, Ward, and Ma.[29] The Known Item results for Carnegie Mellon (28%) compare well with the Finding specific library materials category (33.2%) reported by Kibbee, Ward, and Ma,[30] but Sears' categories didn't offer a comparison.[31] The Facts/Ready Reference results for Carnegie Mellon of 19% compared well with 22.2% Ready Reference for Sears,[32] but Kibbee, Ward and Ma only reported 9.1%.[33] For Reference results, Carnegie Mellon's 19% is close to Kibbee, Ward, and Ma's 20.2% Subject base [sic] research,[34] but Sears reported 33.3% for the level of Reference questions.[35] Perhaps this is due to some queries identified as Known Item by Carnegie Mellon or Finding specific library materials by Kibbee, Ward and Ma being considered Reference by Sears.

Of the 425 transcripts where an exchange progressed through all three stages of the reference interaction, 155 (37%) contained no question for the Librarian's Response, 197 (46%) contained closed questions, and 73 (17%) contained open questions (with many of the 73 also containing closed questions). This is shown below in Figure 3. At this point, it's important to note that since librarians are asking closed and open questions, reference interviews are occurring. Since questioning occurred in 270 interactions, reference interviews were taking place 64% of the time. This result is quite close to Smyth and Johnston's finding that " . . . 57% of sessions include a reference interview" in their sample of 46 synchronous digital reference interactions.[36] It also compares favorably to the face-to-face rates found by Ross and Nilsen and Dewdney and Ross (from 45% to 51%).[37]

The most surprising finding concerned unfavorable patron responses. The authors expected to find higher levels of unfavorable responses from patrons when librarians asked questions. However, the levels were so low that cross-tabulation would be meaningless. Figure 4 shows the breakdown of the five negative responses received from the 270 transcripts that contained questions from the librarians.

Cross-Tabulated Statistics

As mentioned above, the low levels of unfavorable patron responses left just one relationship to analyze in the cross-tabulated statistical results. This relationship was the Type of Patron Query versus the Librarian Response. Table 1 contains the data used for a chi-square test that was conducted using SPSS software. Of particular interest was the data point of row 4, column 3.

FIGURE 3. Librarian's Response (425 Transcripts Where an Exchange Took Place)

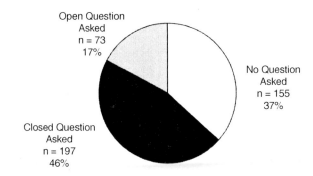

TABLE 1. Type of Patron Query versus Librarian Response

	No Question	Closed Question	Open Question	Total
Directional/Policy/Procedure	n = 65	n = 58	n = 18	n = 141
Known Item	n = 36	n – 73	n = 11	n = 120
Facts/Ready Ref	n = 28	n = 40	n = 14	n = 82
Reference	n = 26	n = 26	n = 30	n = 82
Total	n = 155	n = 197	n = 73	n = 425

FIGURE 4. Level of Negative Response to Librarian's Questioning

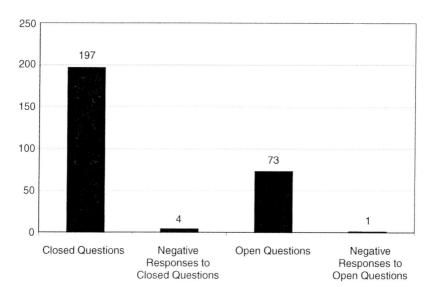

This was the observed value for an open question by the librarian when the patron asked a reference query. The observed value was double the expected value–meaning that open questioning was more prevalent for reference queries than for other types of querying. Overall, the distribution was significant with a *p* of 0.000 for the table.

CONCLUSION

The chief impetus for this study was to examine the perception in the library community that the synchronous digital reference environment is not suitable for conducting a reference interview. This perception could become a self-fulfilling prophecy. In contrast to this perception, the results of this case study indicate that reference interviews occurred 64% of the time with a favorable response by the patron in all but five cases. The Carnegie Mellon results also show that, contrary to popular belief, all types of queries are being posed, not just ready reference. Kibbee, Ward and Ma came to the same conclusion, stating "the range of questions, from simple queries about library hours to questions requiring expert bibliographic sleuthing skills, is not unlike the range of questions received in person,"[38] while Ford's comparison of e-mail, chat and face-to-face interactions led her to conclude that there was "no difference in the proportion of holdings questions, research questions, or requests for evaluation/opinion across media."[39] Based on these findings, the authors would like to offer some encouragement to techno-stressed librarians–the reference interview seems to be alive and well in the brave new world of synchronous digital reference.

FUTURE CONSIDERATIONS

It is clear from the work on this case study that a need exists in the library research community for a common schema or categorization for query types. If a common schema could be developed, this would improve the ability to compare results across different settings. Until then, the authors suggest that their schema could be employed to analyze transcripts from other settings, in different types of libraries, with different user populations, to find out whether synchronous digital reference interviews are taking place.

Another element missing from the research into synchronous digital reference is data on the patron's experience beyond simple measures of satisfaction. For example, how do patrons feel about the pace of the dialogue with the librarian? Is the patron impatiently waiting for a response or are they multitasking? Are patrons able or willing to shift to a face-to-face interaction to better negotiate their information needs? Perhaps focus groups or post-chat surveys of patrons would yield useful results.

NOTES

1. The authors used King's definition: "Questions are open when the response is left up to the respondent; . . . Questions are closed when the respondent does not have a choice in his response other than those provided by the questioner. Two general types of closed questions are those which may be answered 'yes' or 'no' and those which are 'forced-choice' " (this or that). Geraldine B. King, "The Reference Interview: Open & Closed Questions," *RQ* 12 (Winter 1972): 158.

2. Catherine Sheldrick Ross and Kirsti Nilsen, "Has the Internet Changed Anything in Reference?" *Reference & User Services Quarterly* 40, no. 2 (Winter 2000): 150.

3. DIG_REF. Available: <http://www.vrd.org/Dig_Ref/dig_ref.shtml>. livereference. Available: <http://groups.yahoo.com/group/livereference/>. Accessed: July 17, 2002.

4. Karla Hahn, "An Investigation of an E-Mail-Based Help Service," *CLIS TECHNICAL REPORT NO. 97-03* (January 1997) Available: <http://www.clis.umd. edu/research/reports/tr97/03/9703.html>. Accessed: July 17, 2002.

5. Bernie Sloan, *Service Perspectives for the Digital Library: Remote Reference Services.* Available: <http://www.lis.uiuc.edu/~b-sloan/e-ref.html>. Accessed: July 17, 2002.

6. Stephen Francoeur, "An Analytical Survey of Chat Reference Services," *Reference Services Review* 29, no. 3 (2001): 201.

7. Francoeur, 200. See also Linda C. Smith and Lydia E. Harris, "Real-Time Virtual Reference Requires Real-Time Virtual Reference Skills" (paper presented at the 3rd Annual VRD Conference, Orlando, FL, Nov. 2001), Slide 28. Available: <http://www.vrd.org/conferences/VRD2001/proceedings/smithharris.shtml>. Accessed: July 17, 2002.

8. Judith F. Trump and Ian P. Tuttle, "Here, There, and Everywhere: Reference at the Point-of-Need," *Journal of Academic Librarianship* 26, no. 6 (November 2001): 465.

9. Matthew Marsteller and Paul Neuhaus, "Providing Chat Reference Services: A Survey of Current Practices," in *Implementing Digital Reference Services: Setting Standards and Making It Real*, ed. R. David Lankes et al. (New York: Neal-Schuman: 2002).

10. Joanne Smyth and Patricia Johnston, "Preserving Pedagogy in Online Reference" (paper presented at the ILI Conference, London, Mar. 2002), Slide 9. Available: <http://www.internet-librarian.com/presentations/smyth.pps>. Accessed: July 17, 2002.

11. Joseph Janes, "Digital Reference: Reference Librarians' Experiences and Attitudes," *JASIST* 53, no. 7 (March 2002): 554.

12. Janes, 560.

13. Janes, 561.

14. JoAnn Sears, "Chat Reference Service: An Analysis of One Semester's Data," *Issues in Science and Technology Librarianship* 32 (Fall 2001). Available: <http://www.istl.org/istl/01-fall/article2.html>. Accessed: June 12, 2002.

15. William A. Katz, *Introduction to Reference Work: Volume I, Basic Information Services*, 8th ed. (Boston: McGraw-Hill, 2002), 15-19.

16. Sears.

17. Jo Kibbee, David Ward, and Wei Ma, "Virtual Service, Real Data: Results of a Pilot Study," *Reference Services Review* 30, no. 1 (2002): 33.

18. Smyth and Johnston. Available: <http://www.internetlibrarian.com/presentations/smyth.pps>. Accessed: July 17, 2002; Charlotte Ford, "Questions Asked in Face-to-Face, Chat, & E-mail Reference Interactions" (paper presented at the ALA Annual Conference, Atlanta, June 2002. Available: <http://www.ala.org/rusa/mouss/archives/res/forum02/userQs.htm>; Matthew Marsteller and Paul Neuhaus, "The Chat Reference Service Experience at Carnegie Mellon University" (poster session presented at the ALA Annual Conference, San Francisco, June 2001). Available: <http://www.contrib.andrew.cmu.edu/~matthewm/ALA_2001_chat.html>. Accessed: July 17, 2002.

19. Wendy Diamond and Barbara Pease, "Digital Reference: A Case Study of Question Types in an Academic Library," *Reference Services Review* 29, no. 3 (2001): 214-5; Beth A. Garnsey and Ronald R. Powell, "Electronic Mail Reference Services in the Public Library," *Reference & User Services Quarterly* 39, no. 3 (Spring 2000): 250.

20. King, 157-160; Mary Jo Lynch, "Reference Interviews in Public Libraries," *The Library Quarterly* 48, no. 2 (April 1978): 130-31, 135; Marilyn Domas White, "The Dimensions of the Reference Interview," *RQ* 20 (Summer 1981): 377; Peter Ingwersen and Soren Kaae, *User-librarian Negotiations and Information Search Procedures in Public Libraries: Analysis of Verbal Protocols; Final Research Report* (Copenhagen:

Royal School of Librarianship, 1980): 92-102; Brenda Dervin and Patricia Dewdney, "Neutral Questioning: A New Approach to the Reference Interview," 25, no. 4 (Summer 1986): 506, 508; Catherine Sheldrick Ross, "How to Find Out What People Really Want to Know," *The Reference Librarian* 16 (1987): 25-7.

21. Ross and Nilsen.

22. Patricia Dewdney and Catherine Sheldrick Ross, "Flying a Light Aircraft: Reference Service Evaluation from a User's Viewpoint," *RQ* 34, no. 2 (Winter 1994): 226.

23. Ethel Auster and Stephen B. Lawton, "Improving Performance: The Relationship Between Negotiation Behaviors of Search Analysts and User Satisfaction with Online Bibliographic Retrieval," in *Proceedings of the 47th ASIS Annual Meeting*, ed. Raymond F. Vondran et al. (White Plains: Knowledge Industry Publications, 1983): 126-7.

24. Auster and Lawton, "Search Interview Techniques and Information Gain as Antecedents of User Satisfaction with Online Bibliographic Retrieval," *JASIS* 35, no. 2 (1984): 98.

25. Ross and Nilsen, 150.

26. Howard E.A. Tinsley and David J. Weiss, "Interrater Reliability and Agreement," in *Handbook of Multivariate Statistics and Mathematical Modeling*, ed. Howard E.A. Tinsley and Steven D. Brown. (San Diego: Academic Press, 2000).

27. Research Randomizer: Instant Random Sampling and Random Assignment. Available: <http://www.randomizer.org/>. Accessed: November 29, 2001.

28. Sears.

29. Kibbee, Ward and Ma, 33.

30. Kibbee, Ward and Ma, 33.

31. Sears.

32. Sears.

33. Kibbee, Ward and Ma, 33.

34. Kibbee, Ward and Ma, 33.

35. Sears.

36. Smyth and Johnston.

37. Ross and Nilsen; Dewdney and Ross, 226.

38. Kibbee, Ward and Ma, 33.

39. Ford.

APPENDIX A. SCHEMA DEFINITION

Query Type

1 = Directional/Policy/Procedure–Queries that simply ask for directions for where something is physically or virtually located. Queries that pertain to library policies, services or procedures. Requires only knowledge of facilities, systems, policies or procedures to answer.

Directional Examples
Deciphering a catalog record–What does "Location: Stacks-2" mean?
Where is the Web of Science database on the library Web site?
(patron knows the resource they want by name)

Policy/Procedure Examples
Can I check out an item that has "New Book" as a location?
What is "my ID number"?
Do I have to come to the library to check an item out–can't I just send my secretary?

2 = Known Item–Queries that deal with the location of a book or journal, often referred to as a holdings question. Do we have something or don't we? When the known item turns out to be an unknown item in disguise (because of a faulty or incomplete citation), choose "3 = Facts/Ready Ref." Conference proceedings–despite their difficulty, if the patron has a complete citation it should still be a known item because it does not require questioning to tease out the real query.

Known Item Examples
Do you have the screenplay for "The Desk Set"?
Do you have the FLAIRS 97 conference proceedings?

3 = Facts/Ready Reference–Short answer type queries. These would be things that could easily be answered from factual sources such as almanacs, dictionaries, or encyclopedias. The time factor involved is typically very short. Figuring out bad citations should be placed here.

Facts/Ready Reference Examples
Who was president of the U.S. before James Buchanan?
How many automobile accident fatalities were there in West Virginia in 1985 versus 1995?

Where is the database where I can do citation searching? (Requires knowledge of the content of the database, not just how to get to it.)

4 = Reference–Involves significant contemplation, knowledge or instruction on the part of the librarian. Reference questions would include: guidance with finding the right access points for a topic, teaching the steps of the research process, locating hard to find literature, guidance with database choice, location of hard to find data like industry market share, elusive material properties, etc.

Reference Examples
Can you help me find an overview or recent report of the cruise line industry?
Can you help me find the Gibbs free energy of formation for all the various Lanthanum oxides?
How can I find journal articles on extremophiles?
Where on the Web can I find info on U.S. ambassadorships? (Because it involves searching a resource outside of CMU)
Do you have any info on XXXX?

5 = Technical Problem–The phantom chat. Someone seems to connect but they never pose a query. Chat is terminated prematurely due to a technical problem. (System message: Call terminated unexpectedly.)

6 = Librarian Communication/Training–Staff using the software to arrange for shift turnover or to test the software to see if it's indeed working. Obvious practice questions and training sessions. Librarian Communication includes inquiries from librarians outside CMU about the chat reference service.

Librarian Response

1 = No Question–No clarifying or probing question asked.

2 = Closed Question–Question prompts a response of either yes or no, or to pick between two offered choices.

Closed Question Examples
Do you only want articles that are available full-text?
Do you want books or journal articles?

3 = Open Question–Leaves response up to patron. May be phrased as a request.

<u>Open Question Examples</u>
Please tell me more about your topic.
Where have you looked so far?

Patron Response

1 = Favorable–The patron is willing to continue the dialogue. They answer the question, make a statement, ask another question–in other words stay engaged in the interaction.

2 = Unfavorable–Possible traits of unfavorable responses: impatience, anger, rudeness, abrupt termination. (System message: Call terminated normally.)

3 = None/Not applicable–Technical problem, librarian communication, librarian did not ask a question at stage 2 to be responded to.

Additional Notes

We will always ignore system-supplied openers. (Hello, [patron name], how may I help you today?)
We will always ignore closure questions that are followed by termination of the interaction. (Do you need any further help? No, bye.)
All questions outside of normal operating hours are most likely to be librarian communications or testing or training.

Site Search and Instant Messaging Reference: A Comparative Study

Jody Condit Fagan
Christina Desai

SUMMARY. Site search and online reference, using chat or instant messaging, are two new tools for providing electronic reference services in the online environment. This study compares patrons' use of Morris Library's Site Search and Morris Messenger, its online reference service, to analyze their perceptions and the results found with each. Researchers found they are perceived and used in similar ways despite their differing purposes and mechanics. Time of peak use, content and type of queries, and location of users are similar for both tools, whereas length of session and results found were quite different. Many users do not initially realize that Morris Messenger has a human behind the interface, or that Site Search is merely another keyword search engine, limited to library Web pages. The study confirms the need for real time, human help to fill information needs. *[Article copies available for a fee from The Haworth Document Delivery Service: 1-800-HAWORTH. E-mail address: <docdelivery@haworthpress.com> Website: <http://www.HaworthPress.com> © 2003 by The Haworth Press, Inc. All rights reserved.]*

Jody Condit Fagan (jfagan@lib.siu.edu) is Assistant Professor and Social Sciences Librarian, Library Affairs, and Christina Desai (cdesai@lib.siu.edu) is Assistant Professor and Science Librarian, Library Affairs, both at Southern Illinois University, Carbondale, IL 62901-6632.

[Haworth co-indexing entry note]: "Site Search and Instant Messaging Reference: A Comparative Study." Fagan, Jody Condit, and Christina Desai. Co-published simultaneously in *Internet Reference Services Quarterly* (The Haworth Information Press, an imprint of The Haworth Press, Inc.) Vol. 8, No. 1/2, 2003, pp. 167-182; and: *Virtual Reference Services: Issues and Trends* (ed: Stacey Kimmel, and Jennifer Heise) The Haworth Information Press, an imprint of The Haworth Press, Inc., 2003, pp. 167-182. Single or multiple copies of this article are available for a fee from The Haworth Document Delivery Service [1-800-HAWORTH, 9:00 a.m. - 5:00 p.m. (EST). E-mail address: docdelivery@haworthpress.com].

http://www.haworthpress.com/store/product.asp?sku=J136
10.1300/J136v08n01_14

KEYWORDS. Reference services, search engines, online reference, virtual reference, logs, instant messaging, chat

INTRODUCTION

In the fall of 2000, Morris Library at Southern Illinois University, Carbondale overhauled its Web pages and implemented a Web site search engine. As in many libraries, electronic collections had outgrown the Web navigation scheme then in place, and it was hoped that "Site Search," as the search engine was named, would help users find specific library resources and pages within the Web site. The search engine was immediately popular with users, but study of its transaction logs revealed that users did not always understand its scope or purpose.[1] Users often tried to use Site Search as a reference librarian, posing complex questions or topic queries. Although the library offered e-mail reference at the time, there was no live reference help available online amid all the electronic resources.

As a result of the Site Search log study, the library created and implemented an instant messaging reference service, dubbed Morris Messenger. As the transcript log for Morris Messenger grew, it too was analyzed to determine how patrons were using the service and how successful they were.[2] This article compares usage patterns of the two services to determine whether the problems noted in the use of Site Search have been adequately addressed by Morris Messenger.

Today's searchers are increasingly dependent on the Internet to find information. The *Pew Internet and American Life Project* survey of high school students found that 94% of teenagers who have Internet access reported using the Internet for school research. One 15-year old boy said, "without the Internet you need to go to the library and walk around looking for books. In today's world you can just go home and get into the Internet and type in your search term."[3]

Although typing in a search term in a Web search engine almost always generates some type of result, it does not ensure success. In a study of graduate students searching on the World Wide Web, Peiling Wang and Carol Tenopir found that half of the searchers in their study "failed to find an answer or a correct answer." Searching was not often quick, either: on average, students spent 15 minutes searching and visited about 29 sites for each question.[4] Wang and Tenopir's findings resonate with studies of the public's use of Internet search engines such as the 2001 study by Spink, Wolfram, Jansen, and Saracevic, who found that queries "posed by the public are short, not much modified, and very simple in structure," and when they try to incorporate advanced features, "half of them are mistakes."[5] The conclusion of Spink and her colleagues was that in order to adjust to these factors, "a new generation of Web searching tools" is needed. These new tools should somehow encourage people to persist in electronic information seeking.[6]

The Web, however, is not only a source for information but also a place for communication. In the Pew study, 41% of the young adults said they used on-line communication tools like e-mail or instant messaging to contact teachers or classmates about schoolwork.[7]

The library serves the faculty and students of Southern Illinois University, a state university of approximately 21,600 students, including about 17,000 undergraduates. The main campus is in rural southern Illinois, but the library also serves a large number of off campus and distance learning programs. To better serve the diverse needs of these students on and off campus, the library has significantly increased its expenditure on electronic resources. Spending on electronic resources at Morris Library increased from approximately $70,000 in fiscal year 1998 to $500,000 in fiscal year 2001. As electronic access to databases and journals increased, reference traffic in the library went down. This is not surprising, given the recent national downward trend in reference statistics.[8]

With these national and local trends in mind, Morris Library began offering Morris Messenger, an instant messaging reference system, in the summer of 2001. Another impetus was the high number of inappropriate and unsuccessful searches observed when patrons used the library's Web site search.

Previous Studies of Online User Searching

The idea of studying online user searching behavior is far from new; for an excellent bibliography, see Ingrid Hsieh-Yee's 2001 article in *Library and Information Science Research*.[9] This vast field also encompasses transaction log analysis,[10] commonly performed on online catalogs in the 1980s; studies of World Wide Web search engine use;[11] and Web server log and Web site use analysis.[12] These studies examine how people interact with online systems in finding information and bear some similarity to the previous study of Morris Library's Web site search, mentioned above.[13] One problem common to log analyses is the inability to record users' online perceptions of their searches or to determine whether the results satisfy unless a survey or interview is performed. Also, it is often not possible to distinguish one user from the next at a public terminal. The present study of the Morris Library Site Search and Morris Messenger examines users' attempts to find online guidance during the information finding process and is similar to the studies of chat reference now being performed at many universities.[14] Studies of chat reference transcripts allow definitive identification of individual users; online follow-up surveys can measure their perceptions. Also, chat users occasionally express their satisfaction (or frustration) within the conversation itself.

Some background from Web use studies and chat reference studies is helpful in understanding how users see Site Search and Morris Messenger as similar tools.

In Moukdad and Large's examination of WebCrawler search engine logs, the authors concluded that for users,

> the Web is a place, perhaps close to home, where they can ask for anything and get a reply from someone or something that intuitively understands exactly what they want. They are unaware of the fundamental language problems awaiting users of uncontrolled information retrieval systems.[15]

Users aren't particular about whether it is a person or a thing that interacts with them when they are searching online. Moukdad and Large noted that users also don't think much about the format in which they type their information need: "it is sufficient to pose a question, whether submitted as a single broad term or a convoluted interrogative question, and await an intelligent response."[16] In our experience with Morris Messenger and Site Search, we found that users of both tools used both single terms or phrases and more elaborate questions or sentences.

Morris Messenger and Site Search

Morris Messenger and Site Search have many features in common. Both use an input box for a query and both are located on the library's home page. Both are labeled as to their function, and the input box for Morris Messenger has explanatory text nearby, but otherwise they look much the same to a new user. Both make use of the Internet and as such, lead to the expectation of "type and click" ease and instant results. As with any Internet search engine there are no obvious rules for what kind of query can be entered. Users can enter anything from a single word to a long complete sentence or question in natural language. They can, but rarely do, enter a complex Boolean query. Spelling is creative and far from standard. Because of the ubiquity of text input boxes and search engines on the Internet and the similarity in the appearance of Site Search and Morris Messenger, it is not surprising that some patrons confuse the two.

The similarity ends when the patron enters a query. In Morris Messenger, a chat window pops to the top of both the patron's and librarian's screens. Librarians try to provide a quick and welcoming acknowledgment of the query to assure the patron that personalized help is at hand. At this point, the librarian may provide an immediate answer, ask further questions to clarify the query, or let the patron know that the answer may take a few minutes. While Site Search points users to library Web pages and electronic resources through a computer-generated result display, Morris Messenger allows staff to address any information need with interactivity. Patrons can and do ask all kinds of reference questions. The service is displayed on the home page and in the footer of every other Morris Library Web page when a librarian is online so that patrons may get help at any point in their research. Failed searches in Site Search prompt the patron to try Morris Messenger and about 14% of Morris Messenger queries do originate from Site Search.

METHODOLOGY

An enhanced transaction log of the Morris Library Site Search was kept for just over a month in the fall semester of 2000. Using Perl scripts, researchers recorded the date and time of each search, the search terms, the IP address, the number of hits for Web pages, resources, and journals, what the user selected from the result list, and at what time the user selected results. If a user returned to the result list using the browser's "back" button and selected another result, that was recorded as well. Recording the IP address was useful for identifying unique users (defined as the same IP address searching within a five-minute time frame) and for determining if the user was a library, on-campus, campus network, or out-of-network user.

To study the usage of chat reference, researchers examined conversations from June 12, 2001 to September 19, 2001 to determine how similar Morris Messenger conversations were to Site Search queries. Training and testing conversations were excluded. If an initial instant messaging reference query was neither a statement nor a question, it was marked as similar to search engine style queries. Researchers also noted the degree of interactivity of users who entered search engine type entries into Morris Messenger, and whether their query would have gotten any results in Site Search. So the two tools could be compared, Fall 2001 log data from Site Search was also used to supplement the previous Site Search study.

RESULTS

Overall Usage

While Morris Messenger is available only from 1:00 p.m. to 4:00 p.m., Monday through Friday, Site Search is available 24 hours a day, seven days a week. The weekly usage over the fall 2001 semester for Site Search and Morris Messenger is shown in Figures 1 and 2, respectively. Daily use of Morris Messenger and Site Search is positively correlated; as the use of Site Search grew heavier over the semester, the use of Morris Messenger also grew. This correlation is significant at the 0.01 level (2-tailed; Pearson correlation = 0.332).

Morris Messenger was offered on weekday afternoons based on the hourly usage statistics of Site Search. As Figure 3 shows, the peak hours of Site Search use are from 1:00 p.m. to 4:00 p.m. Although there are other times of high use, and the library has experimented with extended hours, there is not sufficient staff to maintain the service for any but peak hours.

Morris Messenger usage increased from one to two questions per hour in its first semester, Summer 2001, to between two and three questions per hour in Fall 2001 and Spring 2002. An additional 3 patrons per hour got busy signals, since staffing permits only one librarian online. For comparison purposes, physical desk reference traffic averages between 4 and 6.5 questions per hour at each of the six divisional reference desks in the library.

Length of Sessions

The average length of Morris Messenger conversations in Fall 2001 was ten lines, i.e., a total of ten "utterances" by librarian and patron in one conversation. Site Search users usually entered only one query per Site Search session, although those who tried multiple queries averaged a higher number of hits per

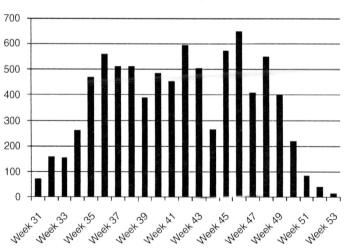

FIGURE 1. Site Searches by Week, Fall 2001

FIGURE 2. Morris Messenger Weekly Usage, Fall 2001

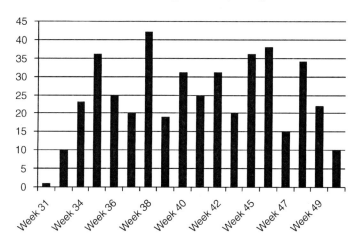

FIGURE 3. Average Site Searches per Hour, Fall 2001

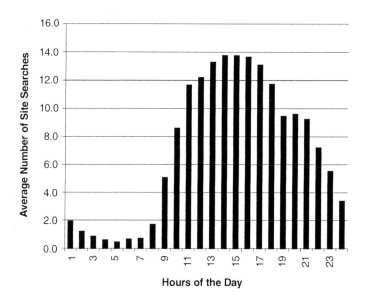

query.[17] The average number of queries per session for the month of the Site Search log study was 1.58.

Location of Users

Users most frequently access both Site Search and Morris Messenger from computers within the library building. Currently, Morris Messenger is limited to the SIU domain to limit the usage, since staff cannot answer all the incoming questions as it is, while Site Search is open to all. Seventy percent of Morris Messenger conversations come from within the library building, while 26% come from computers elsewhere on campus. A small fraction of distance learning students, who are given the Morris Messenger URL, account for 1.5% of its users. (The remaining percentage comes from testing and training questions.) Site Search receives 61% of its queries from in-house machines. Seventeen percent of its queries come from computers elsewhere on campus, and 20% come from off campus.[18]

Content of Query

In analyzing Site Search transaction logs, researchers observed two types of queries: some users were looking for a specific resource, such as a library database, a Web page, or a book title, while others were searching for information on a topic, such as unwed mothers or herbal medicines. Researchers also noted whether Morris Messenger patrons were looking for specific resources or for topics. The percentages were remarkably similar: 33% of Site Search patrons and 29% of Morris Messenger patrons were trying to find resources, while the majority (67% and 71%, respectively) were looking for information about a topic.

Predictably, Site Searches for topics usually failed, since Site Search is designed to link only to the library's Web pages and to specific resources such as SilverPlatter where subject and other searches may then be conducted. Furthermore, of the Morris Messenger queries that were in search engine style format (defined as a single word or phrase query), 65% would have found no matches in Site Search. Users who were looking for resources would have had better-than-even luck with Site Search, as 62% of them would have found some results in Site Search, while only 26% of those looking for a topic would have found any results with Site Search. Many failures in Site Search can be attributed to spelling errors.

Type of Query

Researchers also examined Morris Messenger transcripts to study the behavior of users who typed in a "search engine" style query of a few words for their initial queries versus those who typed a complete statement or question. Of Morris Messenger conversations, 44% began with a search engine style query, consisting of a single word or phrase, such as "murals" or "CHEM 106." Of these users, 47% interacted with the online librarian, yet 80% of those who typed in a complete question or statement interacted.

Success of Queries

Although it is impossible to tell if a Site Search user found results that were helpful, the log files do show if they found and chose results. With instant messaging reference, it is much easier to tell if a conversation was helpful, since the interaction shows more clearly what the need was and if it was met by the librarian. There is also satisfaction survey data available for Morris Messenger reference and comments by users within some of the conversations.

Half (50%) of the site *searches* found at least one result; of the *users* who found results, 64% selected a result. Online tools (like databases and indexes) seemed to be the most satisfying results: of searches that found at least one online tool, 41% chose one of these as their first selection. Only 34% of users who found a library Web page chose one, and 33% of users who found an e-journal chose an e-journal.[19]

Fourteen percent of Morris Messenger conversations originated from the Site Search page results page itself–including queries that had results and queries that had no results Thirty-nine of these conversations (those between July 19th and September 19th) were studied more closely. A reference librarian evaluated the conversations to determine if they were search engine style queries or full questions or statements, and also whether the query was answered successfully. Twenty-two (56%) were Site Search style entries (one word or phrase queries). Half of these users disconnected without interacting with the online librarian, while the other half interacted and successfully completed the reference transaction. Seventeen queries were full questions or statements; only one-fourth of this group disconnected without interacting and receiving an answer. The remaining three-fourths stayed to have their questions answered.

In an attempt to determine how users changed their queries if at all, in going from Site Search to Morris Messenger (or vice versa), queries were cross-referenced using the date, keywords, and computer IP address of the Morris Messenger patron with corresponding information in the Site Search log. Because the library's computers are used by numerous patrons, a "match" was declared only if the date and time were in close proximity and one or more keywords from the queries matched. We found such matches for thirteen of the 39 Morris Messenger queries that originated from the Site Search page. With a larger sample, an entire study could be done on how users change their queries when going from one tool to another. Only two of the thirteen interesting case studies will be presented here. In both cases, the patron did not substantively change the syntax or content of their query when using the different tools.

In the first case, the patron did two similar searches in Site Search, got no results, and tried a similar, but not exact, query in Morris Messenger:

> 2:44 p.m. Site Search: *Architectural design and floor plans for the Alhambra (no results)*

> 2:45 p.m. Site Search: *Alhambra floor plans (no results)*

> 2:46 p.m. Morris Messenger: *Floor plans and design of the Alhambra*

The full transcript is shown in Figure 4. This patron also responded to the short online survey, indicating that the answers were "very" helpful, that "Online Reference (chat) is a very good way to get help," and commenting that "Jody did a wonderful job" in the free-answer box.

The next case study spans a weekend and a weekday. Although there is no way to verify that the off campus patron searching on Saturday for "Laundry/Dry Cleaning Stores" is the same one who searched from off campus on Monday afternoon, coincidence would otherwise seem too great.

> Saturday, 11:47 a.m.: Site Search *off campus, SIU network*: Laundry/Dry Cleaning Stores

> Monday, 2:40 p.m.: Morris Messenger *off campus, SIU network*: dry cleaning

The full transcript of this conversation is shown in Figure 5. Like the previous patron, this patron was also very interactive and claimed to be satisfied with the experience, filling out the short survey with superlative ratings.

A short survey evaluating Morris Messenger was given online between June 7, 2001, and February 25, 2002. Three hundred and forty people responded; of these, 82% said Morris Messenger is a "very" good method of getting help, while 7% said it was a "fairly" good method of getting help. Eighty-two percent said the answers they received were "very" helpful; 12% said the answers were "somewhat" helpful. In a free-answer box on the survey, 115 of the respondents left comments. The most frequent type of comment on the short survey (33 of the 115 respondents) was a general acclamation of the service, such as "I am really impressed. Great idea. Someone should have

FIGURE 4. Morris Messenger Transcript, Case Study 1

Patron: (2:46:46 pm)	Floor plans and design of the Alhambra
Jody: (2:46:53 pm)	hi there. . .
Jody: (2:47:02 pm)	I'm looking for info on that . . .
Patron: (2:47:28 pm)	Hi, I can't find anything
Jody: (2:47:51 pm)	OK I'm looking in ILLINET Online . . . I might know a few tricks that will help . . .
Patron: (2:48:03 pm)	Thank you
Patron: (2:51:32 pm)	Had any luck yet
Jody: (2:51:51 pm)	okay . . . I am probably not going to be able to guarantee a book contains floor plans . . .
Jody: (2:52:03 pm)	but I have found several books on spanish architecture that contain plates, which may be plans.
Patron: (2:52:14 pm)	that is fine, where
Jody: (2:52:49 pm)	Architecture and ideology in early medieval Spain LOCATION: SIUC 2nd fl-Humanities stacks -- CALL NUMBER: Q. 720.94609021
Jody: (2:52:56 pm)	has 72 pages of plates
Jody: (2:53:08 pm)	and it is available . . . there should be other books about that subject nearby.
Patron: (2:53:32 pm)	Thank you very much

FIGURE 5. Morris Messenger Transcript, Case Study 2

Patron: (2:40:19 pm)	dry cleaning
Jody: (2:40:29 pm)	Hey, how are ya?
Jody: (2:40:57 pm)	are you looking for a local business or for information about dry cleaning? or something else maybe?
Patron: (2:41:20 pm)	good i am trying to search for a book on how to start a laundry/dry cleaning business
Jody: (2:41:53 pm)	neat! if you can hang on for a minute, I might be able to find something for ya . . . .
Patron: (2:42:01 pm)	Ok
Jody: (2:43:30 pm)	we have a book called "business plans handbook" that has many small businesses in it . . . I am going to go look in it and see if it has dry cleaning . . .
Patron: (2:43:51 pm)	ok cool
Jody: (2:45:36 pm)	okay here's the scoop:
Jody: (2:46:44 pm)	the Business Plans Handbook volume 3 does have a section on starting a dry cleaning business (p. 85-105). However this book is in Reference, which means you can't check it out. It is on the 3rd floor , call number q. 658.4012 B9796 v.3
Patron: (2:47:04 pm)	ok thanks
Jody: (2:47:09 pm)	as far as books you can check out, you will probably have to look for books on starting a small business (generic) and then apply them to the world of dry cleaning.
Jody: (2:47:29 pm)	you can print out this transcript if you want after you disconnect.
Patron: (2:47:39 pm)	ok thank you for your help

thought of this a long time ago." Twenty-six of the respondents specifically mentioned "helpfulness," both of particular people and of the service in general ("Very helpful–immediate is great!"). Full results of this survey as well as a report of a longer survey will be found in the August 2002 issue of *Reference Services Review.*[20]

DISCUSSION

Usage

User interactivity in the use of both tools increases the likelihood of getting results. Although Morris Messenger by its very nature allows patrons to be more interactive with their questions, Site Search users often attempt to interact with the system as well. Users who do try multiple queries with Site Search do get more hits and choose more results, indicating that this strategy can make it a more successful tool.

The corresponding patterns of usage of Site Search and Morris Messenger across a semester indicates that Site Search data, which is available all hours of the day, would provide good information on which to plan expanded hours for other online tools. Since Site Search is busiest on weekdays, during the afternoons, and since usage for the two tools is positively correlated, it can be inferred that the initial decision to staff Morris Messenger on weekday afternoons was optimal, given the shortage of staff.

Length of Session

Given the dramatic difference in the average length of sessions of the two tools (1.58 queries in Site Search vs. ten lines of interaction in Morris Messenger), and the very high number of inappropriate and failed Site Search queries, it seems fair to suggest that library researchers' information needs are usually too complex to be expressed in a single word or phrase. Several exchanges between patron and librarian are needed before the information need can be adequately addressed. It should also be noted that patrons, after finding a resource (the most successful search type in Site Search), are still at the beginning of the research process. Having found the appropriate resource, such as Art Abstracts or Zoological Record, they may need additional help to meet the original information need.

Location

Although off-campus users of Site Search are a significant percentage of users, both Morris Messenger and Site Search users are most frequently found in the library building. Since physical reference desk traffic has gone down, but instant messaging reference users are still frequently in the building, this suggests that *place* in the information world is no longer defined by physical structures. Practically speaking, librarians need to have an online presence even if they and their patrons are in the same physical location.

Content and Success of Queries

Clearly, patrons do not know that while search engines are useful for some kinds of queries, human help is more efficient and helpful for investigating a research topic. While searching for the location of a database or a piece of library information (such as fines) can be done effectively with Site Search, topical searches usually fail. In Web search engines, the corpus of information is so much greater that the user gets the appearance of finding information about a topic, but a short time with a reference librarian would greatly reduce the number of false leads found in Web searching.

The fact that users often entered search engine style queries into Morris Messenger shows either that they didn't know a human was behind the interface, or else that they didn't feel the need to phrase their information request differently for an online human. Since most (80%) of those who entered a full statement or a question interacted with the online librarian, but less than half (44%) of those who entered a search engine style query interacted, it seems that many of the latter group just did not know what they were getting into. Faced with an unexpected human presence, they often retreated.

Obviously many of the problems associated with search engines are absent in instant messaging reference. Misspellings, for example, often result in failed searches. One of the most common and most often misspelled queries in Site Search was for SilverPlatter; queries for silverplater, silverplattr, and silvrplatter yielded no results and no alternative spelling suggestions. Spelling difficulties seldom pose any obstacle to understanding in Morris Messenger. Site Search often just doesn't find what the user is looking for; even in Site Searches for resources, the most successful search type, only about 33% to 41% of users selected a resource from a result list. As for searches for research topics, which account for 67% of Site Search queries, results are predictably poor since this tool is not designed to address topic searches at all.

One of the conclusions resulting from a study of the use of the Morris Library Web site search engine was that instant messaging reference would be of great help to users who got "no results" from Site Search. This study confirms that prediction, but only for those who are willing to use the instant messaging tool to interact with the online librarian. Of those referred from Site Search, all of those who interacted with the online librarian (59%) had their questions answered. Of those who understood they were in a different medium and phrased a question or statement as if they were talking to a human, many more (75%) interacted and received answers. Of those who tried Site Search unsuccessfully and re-entered a search engine style query, less than half stayed online and carried the transaction through to successful completion.

CONCLUSION

The popularity of Site Search and the corresponding usage of Morris Messenger suggest that both methods of accessing library information are here to stay. Despite the low success rate with Site Search queries, especially with topic searches, users persist in using it even when they are in the library building. Morris Messenger usage is also high within the library building. Many users seem not to expect the human element and many of those users refrain from interacting with the online librarian. Others grasp the difference between interacting with a search engine and interacting with a human, and phrase their queries in full sentences as they would in a face-to-face transaction. In either case, those who interact with the online librarian in almost all cases have their questions answered. Poor spelling, lack of library experience, and inarticulateness seldom prevent success in the instant messaging environment. Site Search has the advantage of 24 hour availability, but usage statistics show that most library research is conducted during the day, on weekdays, when Morris Messenger is available. This research confirms Moukdad and Large's observations about Web searchers' expectations (quoted above) and suggests that despite users' faith in online sources, the quality of the answer in an automated system is still very dependent on the quality of the query and the scope of the search engine.

Until now Morris Library has not aggressively marketed Morris Messenger since it has been staffed only on a volunteer basis. With the transition to centralized reference at Morris, it will become a regular part of public services. This research suggests that more marketing is in order, not only to make patrons aware of the service but to educate them about what it is and how it differs from a search engine. Changes to the interfaces of both Site Search and Morris Messenger, followed by usability studies, may eliminate some of the confusion and encourage use.

In general, libraries need to help patrons distinguish between online tools, even those they cannot control, like Internet search engines. Librarians could play a valuable role by clearly defining what users should expect, in content and in timeliness, from e-mail, chat, and physical reference media, and from Internet search engines and individual site search tools.

REFERENCES

1. Jody Condit Fagan, "Use of an Academic Library Web Site Search Engine," *Reference & User Services Quarterly* 41, no. 3 (Spring 2002): 244-252.

2. Christina M. Desai, "Instant Messaging Reference: How Does It Compare?" *The Electronic Library* 21 (2003): 21, no. 1: Jody Condit Fagan and Margie Ruppel, "Instant Messaging Reference: User Evaluation of Library Chat," *Reference Services Review* 30, no. 3 (August 2002): 183-197.

3. Amanda Lenhart, Maya Simon, and Mike Graziano, *The Internet and Education: Findings of the Pew Internet and American Life Project* (Washington, DC: Pew Internet & American Life Project, 2002). Available: <http://www.pewinternet.org>. Accessed: July 1, 2002.

4. Peiling Wang and Carol Tenopir, "An Exploratory Study of Users' Interaction with World Wide Web Resources: Information Skills, Cognitive Styles, Affective States, and Searching Behaviors," in *Proceedings of the National Online Meeting, May 12-14, 1998.* (Medford, NJ: Information Today, 1998): 445-454.

5. Amanda Spink, Dietmar Wolfram, Bernard J. Jansen, and Tefko Saracevic, "Searching the Web: The Public and Their Queries," *Journal of the American Society for Information Science and Technology* 52, no. 3 (February 2001): 233-234.

6. Ibid., 234.

7. Lenhart, Simon, and Graziano, 4.

8. ARL Statistics, *Service Trends in ARL Libraries, 1991-2000.* Available: <http://www.arl.org/stats/arlstat/graphs/2000t1.html>. Accessed: July 2, 2002.

9. Ingrid Hsieh-Yee, "Research on Web Search Behavior," *Library and Information Science Research*, 23 no. 2 (2001): 167-185.

10. Thomas A. Peters, Martin Kurth, and Neal K. Kaske, "Transaction Log Analysis," *Library Hi Tech Bibliography* 8 (1993): 151-83; *Library Hi Tech* 11, no. 2 (1993): (entire issue).

11. Bernard J. Jansen, Amanda Spink, J. Bateman, and Tefko Saracevic, "Real Life Information Retrieval: A Study of User Queries on the Web," *SIGIR Forum* 32, no. 1 (1998): 5-17; Bernard J. Jansen, Amanda Spink, and Tefko Saracevic, "Failure Analysis in Query Construction: Data and Analysis from a Large Sample of Web Queries," in *Digital Libraries: The Third ACM Conference on Digital Libraries*, (New York: Association for Computing Machinery; 1998): 289-290; Bernard J. Jansen, Amanda Spink, and Tefko Saracevic, "Real Life, Real Users, and Real Needs: A Study and Analysis of User Queries on the Web," *Information Processing and Management* 36, no. 2 (2000): 207-27.

12. David Nicholas, Paul Huntington, Peter Williams, Nat Lievesley, Tom Dobrowlski and Richard Withey, "Developing and Testing Methods to Determine the Use of Web Sites: Case Study Newspapers," Aslib Proceedings 51, no. 5 (1999): 144-54; Patrick T. McGlamery, "MAGIC Transaction Logs as Measures of Access, Use, and Community," *The Journal of Academic Librarianship* 23 (1997): 505-10.

13. Fagan, 244-252.

14. Fagan and Ruppel, 183-197. Desai, 21-24; JoAnn Sears, "Chat Reference Service: An Analysis of One Semester's Data," *Issues in Science & Technology Librarianship*. no. 32 (Fall 2001). Available: <http://www.istl.org/01-fall/index.html>. Accessed:

July 7, 2002; Kelly M. Broughton, "Our Experiment in Online, Real-Time Reference, *Computers in Libraries* 21, no. 4 (2001): 26-31; Linda Eichler and Michael Halperin, "LivePerson: Keeping Reference Alive and Clicking," *EContent* 23, no. 3 (June/July 2000): 63-66; Sam Stormont, "Going Where the Users Are: Live Digital Reference," *Information Technology & Libraries* 20, no. 3 (September 2001): 129-134.

15. Haidar Moukdad and Andrew Large, "Users' Perceptions of the Web as Revealed by Transaction Log Analysis," *Online Information Review* 25, no. 6 (2001): 357.

16. Ibid., 357.

17. Fagan, 249.

18. Ibid., 247.

19. Ibid, 248-249.

20. Fagan and Ruppel, 183-197.

Index

24/7 Reference, 39,45,111-112